T0277309

STOWAWAY

STOWAWAY

The Disreputable Exploits of the Rat

Joe Shute

BLOOMSBURY WILDLIFE

LONDON • OXFORD • NEW YORK • NEW DELHI • SYDNEY

BLOOMSBURY WILDLIFE
Bloomsbury Publishing Plc
50 Bedford Square, London, WC1B 3DP, UK
29 Earlsfort Terrace, Dublin 2, Ireland

BLOOMSBURY, BLOOMSBURY WILDLIFE and the Diana logo are trademarks
of Bloomsbury Publishing Plc

First published in the United Kingdom in 2024

A catalogue record for this book is available from the British Library

Library of Congress Cataloguing-in-Publication data has been applied for

ISBN: HB: 978-1-399-40250-7; ePub: 978-1-399-40249-1; ePDF: 978-1-399-40254-5

2 4 6 8 10 9 7 5 3 1

Typeset in Bembo Std by Deanta Global Publishing Services, Chennai, India
Printed and bound in Great Britain by CPI Group (UK) Ltd, Croydon CR0 4YY

To find out more about our authors and books visit www.bloomsbury.com
and sign up for our newsletters

For Molly and Ermintrude,
my friends among rogues

Contents

Rats, rats, rats! Hundreds, thousands, millions of them, and every one a life.

R. M. Renfield, Bram Stoker's *Dracula*

CHAPTER ONE

Devil's Lapdog

Rat stories are like ghost stories: everybody has one. This is mine. It is a cold April morning and I am parked in an alley in Openshaw, Manchester, one row back from a main road lined with takeaways, corner shops and a couple of shisha cafés. At the near end of the alley is an entrance leading to some flats upstairs. Extra panels are nailed into the battered door, which looks as if somebody has previously kicked it in.

The alley is strewn with rubbish: broken bottles of miniatures, sheets of splintered plywood, an abandoned shopping trolley and a zipped, bulging, pink suitcase. There is also a plastic industrial waste bin on wheels behind a Chinese takeaway. I see a man swing open a back door from the takeaway and chuck in a few refuse bags, before locking it and walking back inside. He is on autopilot, oblivious to me and the many other pairs of eyes watching from the shadows.

A van pulls up alongside me and a middle-aged man with a scruffy grey beard, wearing a black cap, jumper and jeans and a high-vis vest, steps out. I can hear his dogs whining in the back. After exchanging greetings he warns me that when he releases them they might be a bit 'boisterous'. He is Martin Kilbride, social worker turned rat-catcher and one of the last of his ancient profession in Britain still to operate using ratting dogs (in his case, a pair of Manchester terriers). Peering down the alley, he briefs me on the scene.

A few weeks previously one of the tenants in the flat above the shops complained to his landlord that so many rats had colonised the alley they were running over his feet whenever he stepped outside. Martin was telephoned and after scoping out from the same place where I have been waiting, he noticed the rats streaming out of a Honda Jazz car abandoned in a nearby side street and climbing into the bin to feast on the Chinese takeaway food dumped there each day.

The rats had made their way into the car through the exhaust and established a colony in its engine bay, Martin tells me. When I ask how they had got into the large bin, as I had just seen the man lock the top of it, he says that is simple: they chew through the heavy-duty moulded plastic from the bottom. Rats, after all, are an animal that can gnaw through concrete.

Since then, the rat-infested car has been towed and Martin has left some live traps baited with chunks of bread at various points where he suspects the colony might have relocated. Now it is time to inspect the catch. He attaches his pair of terriers, Drake and Izzy, to a lead and walks down the alley. I follow behind gripped with a rising sense of dread. Do I really want to watch these dogs tear another living animal to pieces, I ask myself? Martin has shown me some videos on his phone of the dogs tossing a live rat up like a rag doll and it makes a hideous sight. The dogs begin to strain at the leash and I hope the rats have heard us coming.

Manchester terriers were specially bred for ratting and rabbit-coursing and were known as 'the gentleman's terrier' in Victorian Britain. Black and tan with smooth hair and pointed ears, their earliest appearance in the written record as being used for ratting comes from Dr John Caius, physician to several members of the royal family over the course of the sixteenth century, including Queen Elizabeth I.

Martin proudly boasts that the legendary Victorian rat-catcher Jack Black, who became a nineteenth-century celebrity known for his green coat, scarlet waistcoat and rat belt buckle, also hunted his quarry using Manchester terriers (as well as a team of ferrets). Jack Black was famous for being able to plunge his hand into a cage full of live rats and emerge unscathed. It was not always so, his skin was covered in the scars of old rat bites.

As we watch the dogs at work, Martin points out where they have evolved brown spots near their eyes as a defence mechanism to confuse rats attempting to bite them. I notice the dogs also have a curious habit of jerking backwards every few moments as they sniff cracks in the brickwork and dive through piles of rubbish. Martin tells me this is another survival technique ingrained in the dogs, because when it is cornered, a rat always strikes first.

As we work down to the far end, a man walks into the alley with a jerky gait and the glint of an addict in his eyes. There is enough drug detritus around to suggest this is a well-used spot and the moment he sees us he veers back out and onto the main road. He keeps his distance until the natural flow of alley life resumes.

Our search concludes at a drain-hole cover. Drake begins to yelp and sniff, shoving his snout into the gaps between the iron bars. Peering into the darkness below, Martin tells me the rats will have beat a hasty retreat into the sewer. 'The thing about Drake's nose is he's never wrong,' he says. I am relieved that things have concluded in this uneasy truce: the rat-catcher having chased the vermin away and his quarry regrouping underground, waiting for the next opportunity to re-emerge.

Rats represent the worst of us, or at least that is what we tell ourselves. They are rapacious, over-sexed, destructive, pestilent – hideous enough to justify spreading poison around our streets and homes and releasing a pair of hounds down an alley in pursuit of blood. We are obsessed as a society with the notion of rats mustering in the gloom and waiting to invade our lives. Newspapers are sporadically filled with stories of super-rats growing immune to poison and ever more bloated on our waste. I know, because as a journalist I have written some of these stories myself.

In 1813, the Yorkshire-born journalist Charles Fothergill (who later relocated to Canada) attempted some brief arithmetic on rat reproduction. He calculated that left to their own devices, a single pair of rats would produce 3 million young during their three-year lifespan. Fothergill concluded that 'the whole surface of the earth in a very few years would be rendered a barren and hideous waste, covered with myriads of famished grey rats, against which man himself would contend in vain'.

This is the sort of dodgy mathematics that has led to the old adage you are never more than 6 feet away from a rat, or that there is a rat for every person in Britain. In short, nobody knows the true number. Much of what is floating around the internet is peddled by the pest-control industry itself, which clearly has a vested interest in an over-inflated public perception of the threat rats pose. Estimates of the number of rats in Britain ranges from 10.5 million to in excess of 200 million. Most experts point towards the former as a more accurate representation. Loosely (although some will argue with this), it is supposed there are about 3.5 million urban rats and about 7 million rural rats. Britain's human population is around 67 million, meaning we outnumber rats by more than six to one.

Despite our best efforts to tarnish their reputation it is, of course, humans who are far more culpable for the rapid destruction of the earth. Rats, like many animals we brand as 'vermin', thrive as a direct result of the way we live and interact with the land, a mirror reflecting back to us our worst excesses.

Could we define this as a symbiotic relationship? Certainly it is obvious why rats have evolved so successfully to live alongside humans. But what do we gain from the rats? An easy scapegoat, perhaps, an object of fascination and folklore that reveals to us the darker aspects of the human condition. Rats are in many ways a shadow of us – something to be engrossed by and horrified by in equal measure. And yet a definition of irrational fear is to be scared of your own shadow.

Normally, we live in a state of hidden enmity. The rats have carved up colonies, breeding and feeding grounds under our feet which they defend just as jealously as we do our own. Rats exist in the corners of our minds and the borders of human consciousness. But occasionally – and often in moments of great human drama, be it fire, flood, war or plague – the rats rise up.

So it was during the coronavirus pandemic. Suddenly, it seemed, people were seeing rats everywhere. In *The Plague*, the 1947 dystopian novel by Albert Camus, the first sign that a lethal disease had gripped the Algerian port city of Oran is when the rats begin to stream out from the sewers and die in the streets in their thousands. Covid-19 elicited a similar phenomenon. While our cities locked down and restaurants and takeaways shuttered their doors, the urban population of rats was deprived of its usual food source. Forced to seek out new feeding grounds, the starving rats went on the march.

Around the time of the first lockdown, when I met Martin in the Manchester alley, there were flurries of reports of rats burrowing into cellars, clambering up drainpipes and colonising compost bins. Rat-catchers like Martin had experienced a surge in call-outs to homes and businesses being besieged by rats as the lack of litter forced them out into the open.

In some quarters of the press and on social media something akin to moral panic ensued. The rats were reportedly heading out from inner cities and into suburbia – as if Britain's leafier streets had somehow previously been rat-free locations. With humans absent from office blocks, rats had taken over, building new colonies above the polystyrene ceiling tiles, stripping computer cables and nesting in desk drawers. Rats also followed us out to our local parks, skittering over the boggy ground churned by all of our feet on our allotted daily walk. Yet all these new sightings were in truth little more than an indication of our own world being in flux. The rats were simply following as we changed our routines, adapting to us. It is what they have done for millennia.

There are two rat emojis in popular use, just as there are two rats in each of our minds. The first is the white laboratory rat (also used for a mouse), harmless and sanitised; an animal that has sacrificed more in the pursuit of understanding the human condition than any other and to which countless lives are owed. The second is the wild brown rat, long cited as a symbol of societal decay. The lab rat marks progress; the wild rat humanity's descent and the long-standing popular fear that we will one day cast aside moral laws and devolve into a rat-like society.

One popular nineteenth-century description of the rat, which persists today, is 'the devil's lapdog'. In his book *Rat*, Jonathan Burt makes the point that rats represent a hefty slice of the seven deadly sins (though nobody could ever accuse the industrious rodent of sloth). 'The rat,' he writes, 'is the agent of human dissolution'.

In 1947, during the post-war baby boom when overpopulation was becoming a source of wider concern, the US research psychologist John B. Calhoun started conducting crowding experiments with rats. Calhoun's neighbour agreed to let him build a quarter-acre enclosure in disused woodland behind his Maryland home, a pen he nicknamed 'rat city'.

The habitat, Calhoun imagined, was sufficient to accommodate 5,000 rats, and to kick things off he introduced five pregnant females. Brown rats can produce litters of 14 pups, and average around half a dozen. Given their ability to fall pregnant almost immediately after giving birth and gestate while simultaneously lactating, he presumed the woodland floor would soon be teeming. However, despite providing a constant supply of food over two years of research, the population never exceeded 200 and ultimately levelled off at around 150.

A few years later, while employed at the National Institute of Mental Health, Calhoun repeated the experiment but this time in indoor pens that could be viewed by the scientists from above. Once more he introduced rats and provided food, water and bedding. Everything, in other words, a rat could possibly need. Calhoun called this experimental world a 'rat utopia'.

But there was one limit deliberately imposed on this world that was different to his outdoor experiment: space. The rodents bred prodigiously and the pens soon heaved with animals. Then something strange occurred: the rat society started to collapse in upon itself. Dominant males formed aggressive packs that attacked females and the young. Some rats became exclusively homosexual, others hypersexual, attempting to mate with everyone they encountered. Mothers abandoned and even attacked their pups as infant mortality rose to 96 per cent. Cannibalism was rife. What became left of rat utopia was a group of terrified subordinate rodents huddled together for safety in the middle of the pen while the more feral inhabitants of the colony roamed the perimeter. The population crashed and did not recover.

Published in 1962, Calhoun's study came at a time of rapid urban expansion when architects were designing new high-rise buildings and cities in the sky. Calhoun termed his findings of the rats' descent into vice and destruction a 'behavioural sink'. This was a horror story that resonated deeply in an increasingly urbanising society.

Calhoun's rat study is ever-present in science fiction – the idea of humanity living in an overcrowded wasteland and one day turning in upon itself. The cult 1993 film *Demolition Man* envisages a future in 2032 where society has split into two tiers. The rich live above ground in pleasure palaces, drive electric cars and are too squeamish of contact to even have sex. The poor live largely out of sight in underground burrows and emerge only to conduct occasional raids. For food in this subterranean wasteland they eat rat burgers, consuming the animal they have effectively become.

These comparisons sit uncomfortably with us all. Rat is an insult; a verb as well as a noun. The dishonest rat each other out. When cornered, the morally culpable turn upon each other like rats in a sack. The Victorian author and chronicler of rats James Rodwell invites his reader to slowly pronounce the word aloud, R-A-T, savouring the disgust in every letter.

If rat is a dirty word, then so too is vermin. To me it is the worst of human hubris that we choose to deem which animals are acceptable and which are not. Our destructive history and the fact we are currently presiding over the sixth mass extinction should surely give us pause for thought about our assumed dominion.

The Tudor Vermin Acts marked a nadir of this mindset, when successive acts introduced by Henry VIII and Elizabeth I compelled every man, woman and child in the country to kill as many creatures as possible from a designated list of 'vermin'. Hedgehogs, otters, frogs, bullfinches, sparrows and kingfishers were among the multitude of targeted species as well as rats, with bounties for their dead bodies administered by local churchwardens. The acts were finally repealed in the eighteenth century when the impact on Britain's fauna was becoming clear. But the rat bounties continued well into the twentieth century when Rat and Sparrow Clubs would organise regular hunts and collect up the tails for a penny a piece. Such ratting clubs remain in existence today.

Rats, of course, survived the Vermin Acts and the hunting clubs, just as they have done with everything else humans have ever thrown at them. They are in many ways the definitive synanthropic species, occupying a grey area somewhere between the domestic and the wild. They are the ultimate transgressors, slipping between and gnawing through human-defined boundaries and borders. Living in proximity to us, exploiting us, and yet always remaining just outside our control.

Rather than seek to better understand the rat and change our perceptions of what is a fascinatingly complex creature in its own right – as has been done with that other scavenger, the urban fox – we instead condemn rats to the shadows. And in this book that is where I intend to go and find them. If not to rehabilitate, then at least to re-evaluate our relationship with the rat.

It would be customary at this point to tell you about my own personal love for rats, but I wouldn't call it that. While I can happily handle spiders and snakes, feed a feral pigeon on my shoulder and long to stroke the soft fur of the squirrels scampering about my garden, for much of my life rats have made my skin crawl.

Aged 18, I spent a few months working as an English teacher in Ho Chi Minh city in Vietnam and lodged with a local family who had an apartment at the end of a fruit market. At night as I returned home, the headlight of my motorbike taxi would illuminate the alley and the huge rats lumbering past, feasting on whatever had been dropped on the floor from the stalls. The front gate was locked from the inside and it would always take me a few minutes to reach in and open it up. Sometimes, as I jangled the keys in my sweaty hand, I would feel the bristles of a rat's matted fur brush against my leg.

In one shared house in Leeds where I lived in my early twenties, there was a chicken pen in the garden which had become overrun with rats. When you walked around it, the earth was spongy with the network of tunnels beneath the soil. It was a daily occurrence to see a rat lope across the lawn. Living among the colony was a particularly large blonde rat which seemed to terrify even the local cats. I wondered if it might be the king rat, the dominant rodent in every colony? This notion of a rat patriarch to which the others are subservient was first noted in Conrad Gessner's zoological encyclopedia, *Historia animalium*, published in the mid sixteenth century: the one rat to rule them all.

When my wife, Liz, and I moved into our house in Sheffield a few years ago, we soon discovered there was a rat run of interlinked tunnels through the back gardens. They lived under people's sheds and outdoor toilets and tunnelled under the 120-year-old brick walls separating our gardens. One neighbour had reportedly accidentally once dug into a burrow, sending a colony boiling out. A few days later she spotted one of the larger members of the exiled colony swinging from her bird feeders.

One night after returning home from holiday, we were having dinner in the kitchen when we heard a strange scraping coming from one of the cupboards. Inside was half a butternut squash with sizeable tooth marks in the orange flesh, a demolished bag of brown rice and a scattering of raisin-sized rat poos. We discovered the rats had tunnelled into our cellar and been clambering up in between the joists into our kitchen to feed. I plugged the gaps with steel wool (a substance rats abhor), set a few traps under the cupboards and spent several sleepless nights with rats scuttling through my thoughts.

The first trap was sprung a few days later, spraying rat blood on the floor but with no animal in sight. When a stench of decay drifted up from below, we presumed it had retreated into the cellar to die. Eventually, the second trap was sprung. I discovered this rat perfectly preserved in the moment when the trap had snapped. Its fur was clean, belly spotless white and maroon eyes glazed over. The metal trap had broken its neck and a small trickle of blood came out of its yellowed rodent teeth.

Some time afterwards, I killed another rat. We keep chickens in our garden, an animal that offers a constant attraction for rats, and one day found a fresh tunnel had been dug into their coop. Fearful of a colony developing similar to the one in Leeds I mentioned, I once more set a trap with a blob of crunchy peanut butter sprinkled with chicken pellets and placed at the entrance to the tunnel. For good reason rats are neophobic − inherently suspicious of anything new − but eventually it could not resist the bait any longer. The trap did not catch it cleanly and by the time I came out the injured rat had disappeared.

I found it a day later, or to be precise our chickens did, circling the wounded creature as it foraged for fallen seeds under our bird feeder. The rat was clearly struggling to see out of its left eye and was moving slowly with a limp. I watched it staggering around the garden, sticking closely to the wall as is a rat's nature, its long grey tail dragging dejectedly in the leaf litter. At one point it stumbled and fell into our pond. Even considering its dire condition, it still broke out in an effortless rat stroke to get to the other side.

I had never been able to look at a live rat for so long before. Normally any encounters would be a quick flash in front of me as my footsteps sent the rodents skittering in the undergrowth or diving for safety into a rat hole. Watching the animal up close, I noticed its long handsome whiskers and glossy chestnut coat; it had clearly been fattening up on the chicken pellets. Every few seconds it would stop and clean itself, rubbing its paws over its snout and ears, something I later discovered is a behavioural trait when rats are ill at ease.

I was gripped by a sense of guilt about my actions. Watching this poor rat in such a helpless state, I realised how much my perceptions of the animal had been shaped by my own fears rather than the reality. When was I told that it was OK, indeed expected of me, to kill a rat? When exactly do we learn as children that some animals are more equal than others? Some are cute and encouraged to live in our homes and some must be expunged at all costs.

The eighteenth-century Chinese poet Shi Daonan is credited with being the first person to associate rats with human plague. He was 36 and living in China's Yunnan province when one day dying rats started to be found in people's homes, a portent of plague to come. In a poem entitled 'Death of Rats' he wrote:

Rats die in the east,
Rats die in the west.
People look upon the dying rats
As if they were tigers.
A few days following the death of the rats,
People die like city walls.

Today, every schoolchild in Britain is taught that rats are dirty and the direct cause of the Black Death that devastated Europe in the fourteenth century, claiming an estimated 25 million lives due to the fleas carried on their fur. Just 2–4mm in length (around the size of a rat claw), the oriental rat flea, *Xenopsylla cheopis*, remains the most notorious of the more than 2,500 species of flea known around the world, thanks to it being a particularly effective vector of plague. When infected, its digestive system becomes blocked and it vomits the bacteria into anything else it bites. However, it is just one of around 80 fleas harboured by a whole host of mammals which can carry – and transmit – the plague bacterium *Yersinia pestis*. Outbreaks can occur when there are no rats present whatsoever.

A 2018 study of Black Death mortality data conducted by researchers in Norway and Italy has recently contested the dominant narrative that black rats were solely to blame for the plague. The researchers claimed the speed at which the disease spread meant human-borne fleas and lice were more likely responsible for causing so many millions of deaths.

The human flea, *Pulex irritans*, and other ectoparasites are similarly effective at spreading the disease. This remains an issue of deep concern to public health professionals in parts of the world still battling with regular outbreaks of the plague. In a recent study, *Yersinia pestis* was discovered in a high density of human-borne fleas collected from plague-affected villages in Tanzania and Madagascar.

Another study, published in the prestigious journal *Proceedings of the National Academy of Sciences* in 2015, argued that the Black Death came from gerbils in Asia, rather than rats. By analysing tree rings to determine climatic patterns at the time the plague originated, the researchers concluded that the warm and wet weather in Asia would have been ideal for large packs of giant gerbils to thrive – meaning boom time for their fleas, which then could leap onto human and other mammalian reservoirs.

It would be disingenuous to suggest that rats are not a pest and, in the right circumstances, a threat. It would, in fact, be difficult to envisage a more effective harbinger of pestilence than the rat: muscular, ferocious, with incisors that are stronger than steel and bodies capable of squeezing through the tiniest of gaps to access food sources in our homes.

Rats, along with other rodents, pilfer one-fifth of the world's food harvest and can be a reservoir of pathogens known to cause more than 70 diseases. Bubonic plague, cholera, typhus, leptospirosis, cowpox and hantavirus infection have all been traced to rats. A 2014 study from Columbia University found the average New York City subway rat carried 18 novel viruses not yet detected in humans, along with dozens of familiar pathogens. While Covid-19 has so far largely been blamed on bats, rats are feared to be likely carriers of whichever as yet unidentified disease might become the next pandemic.

And yet, despite this feared capacity to bring about our ruin, paradoxically rats have contributed more to the cause of human health than arguably any other species. Ever since the first laboratory rats were used in fasting studies by physiologists in 1828, rats have been continually experimented upon to advance our own interests. The biological similarity to people, the intelligence and sheer toughness of rats, means they are an ideal candidate for experimentation. In 2004, the rat became the third mammal in history to have its genome fully mapped by scientists, following humans and mice. This mapping found almost all human genes known to be associated with diseases have counterparts in the rat genome, with a high degree of genomic and physiologic similarities between the two species. And also that rats are evolving at a far greater speed, roughly three times faster than humans.

The rat involved in the sequencing study was a Norway rat, otherwise known as the brown rat, or sewer rat, alongside other less favourable nomenclature. It was named in the mistaken belief that the rat arrived in Britain via ships transporting lumber from Norway, although the rat actually originated in northern China. There remains some dispute about when it first arrived in the west, but over the course of the eighteenth century it took advantage of the rapid expansion of international trade to become established all over the world. Now found on every continent except Antarctica, where humans have gone, rats have followed, making them one of the most populous and successful mammals on earth. Nearly the most destructive, too. Although that particular mantle belongs to us.

In spite of our eradication efforts, the Norway rat continues to thrive – and grow. Typically measuring between 25cm and 50cm snout to tail and weighing between 200g and 300g, some rats have been recorded as exceeding that. In 2018, a Bournemouth-based pest controller, Terry Walker, who also hunts with a Manchester terrier, caught a rat behind a row of shops measuring 53cm from head to tail (roughly the size of a small cat). It is, he gleefully told a journalist around the time of its capture, only a matter of time before a 2-foot rat (61cm) is caught.

The idea of the monster rat looms large in our cultural consciousness, a creature engorged by our own excess. In his 1983 book, *More Cunning than Man*, writer Robert Hendrickson lists the many similarities between our two species, including our adaptability, omnivorous diets and ferocity, as well as a shared 'irresponsible fecundity in all seasons, with a seeming need to make genocidal war on their own kind'. He describes rats and humans alike as 'utterly destructive, both taking all other living things for their purposes'.

During the First World War, the grossly enlarged trench rats proved almost as horrifying to some as the carnage of the fighting itself. In *Goodbye To All That*, Robert Graves recounts a posting to the French town of Cuinchy, where rats seethed up from a nearby canal to feed on the plentiful corpses. Graves describes the story of a new officer joining the company who on his first night woke in his dugout to discover two rats on his blanket fighting over a severed hand. For four long years during the war, soldiers on all sides lived like rats in 440 miles of tunnels. In his poem 'A Terre', Wilfred Owen mused that the lives of the soldiers and the rats that tormented them were not all that dissimilar, 'nosing along at night' in their subterranean burrows.

Rats succeed where human society has failed. They exploit poor sanitation and housing, and multiply in areas of

environmental vandalism where species-rich habitats have
been turned into monocultures. And above all they are
attracted by the waste of war. They thrived among the
entrenched armies on the Western Front, stealing food scraps
and eating bloated corpses decomposing in shell holes. In
that nightmarish world, the rats too grew crazed by bloodlust.
Various accounts describe rats stripping the flesh off a fallen
soldier and sometimes even attacking the wounded if they
were unable to defend themselves. At night sleeping soldiers
would be awoken by rats scampering across their faces or
attempting to pilfer rations from their pockets. A loathing of
rats unified even mortal enemies. Photographs of German,
French and British soldiers show them proudly exhibiting
the strung-up bodies of rodents they managed to kill in the
trenches.

Rats are a part of war, a manifestation of hatred and
bloodshed. In *Homage to Catalonia*, George Orwell's
biographical account of serving in the Spanish Civil War, he
seems fixated on the rats he encounters. As the historian
D. J. Taylor notes in an essay on Orwell and rats, he is often
more preoccupied with the 'great bloated brutes' than the
fascist enemy he had enlisted to fight.

Over the course of his life, Orwell maintained
something of an obsession with rats. Living on the streets
of Paris and London in the early 1930s he recalled
encounters with vicious rats, including in the kitchen of a
London restaurant chain reputedly so infested that when
he was offered work as a pot washer he was advised to
enter with a loaded revolver. In Orwell's *1984*, rats are used
as an instrument of torture, placed in a cage about
Winston's head in Room 101. Elsewhere in the book the
protagonist Winston is horrified when his partner Julia
tells him how in parts of London rats are now brazenly

attacking children in the street and babies in their cots. 'Of all the horrors in the world,' he muses, 'a rat!'

This terror of rats has in recent history been appropriated by nationalists to dehumanise others. In 1909, the US satirical magazine *Puck* published a cartoon of an Uncle Sam figure as a star-spangled pied piper being followed by a swarm of rats bearing labels such as 'murderer' and 'thief'. The rodents were intended to depict criminally minded immigrants exploiting the country's immigration laws.

Nazi propaganda regularly portrayed Jewish people as rats and *Untermenschen* – an inferior species excluded from any moral code. One front page of the Nazi newspaper *Der Stürmer* carried a cartoon of an officer gassing a colony of dead and fleeing rats at the base of an oak tree. The caption reads: 'When the vermin are dead, the German oak will again flourish.'

In the 1940 Nazi propaganda film *The Eternal Jew*, regular comparisons are made between rats and Jewish people. In one notorious scene, packs of rats are filmed emerging from sewers and chomping through bags of grain, overlaid with shots of the crowded Lodz ghetto, at one stage the second largest established by the Nazis in western Europe with its inhabitants forced into slave labour, starved and shipped out in their tens of thousands to extermination camps. 'Wherever rats appear,' the film narrator declares, 'they bring ruin'.

Given such vicious and loaded comparisons, I started thinking about the literature of my own childhood and the depictions of rats I grew up with. I had presumed the swashbuckling Reepicheep of C. S. Lewis's *Voyage of the Dawntreader* was a rat, but when I researched it discovered he was a mouse. In *Wind in the Willows*, Ratty is a water vole. In the *Redwall* series, written by Brian Jacques, rats were the marauding enemy the mice were forced to defend themselves against.

The vicious rat in Disney's *Lady and the Tramp* terrified me as a child, a greasy, sharp-fanged monster with yellow eyes and a swishing addery tail who sneaks into the baby's room. Even Beatrix Potter, who had her own pet fancy rat called Sammy, cast them in a less than favourable light in her story of a disobedient kitten who escapes up to the attic and is captured by a pair of rats, Samuel Whiskers and his wife, Anna Maria. The rats tie the kitten up and roll it in butter and dough they have stolen from the kitchen intending to turn it into a roly-poly pudding. The kitten, fortunately, manages to escape being eaten. Despite this derogatory depiction of rodent greed, Potter dedicated the story to her pet rat: 'the intelligent pink-eyed representative of a persecuted (but irrepressible) race, an affectionate little friend, and most accomplished thief'.

In search of a more favourable depiction of rats, I turned to a book that had passed me by in childhood, the 1971 classic *Mrs Frisby and the Rats of Nimh*. Written by the *National Geographic* journalist Robert Conly under the pseudonym Robert C. O'Brien, he died aged 55 just two years after the book's publication.

The book tells the story of a field mouse called Mrs Frisby who needs to relocate her children from their winter burrow in a farmer's field before he ploughs the land, but fears her youngest son is too sick to survive the move. In desperation she turns to a colony of rats living under a rose bush on the farm. The rats turn out to be escapees from a mysterious institution called NIMH – where they had been experimented on by scientists and developed extraordinary intelligence as a result. NIMH stands for the National Institute of Mental Health, where John B. Calhoun built his real-life rat utopia and which inspired the story.

The escaped rats occupy an uneasy place in the food chain. Able to read and write, use tools and of comparable intelligence to humans, they are none the more palatable to the farmer, who plans to exterminate them. Instead of a lifetime pilfering from his grain stores, the rats of NIMH dream of a better future where they are self-sufficient and no longer dependent on stealing from human food sources; a place where they can live by a stricter moral code. In one of the many philosophical debates among the colony, one of the rats asks: 'Where does a group of civilised rats fit in?'

As lockdown dragged, a long winter lay ahead of us and with little else on which to focus my mind I thought about Beatrix Potter's eulogy to her fancy rat – a domesticated form of *Rattus norvegicus*. I started looking into it more and discovered a whole world of rat appreciation I never imagined existed, with a National Fancy Rat Society and pedigree shows akin to Crufts.

I wanted the opportunity to study rats up close, to see the characteristics that inspired such antipathy in so many humans and, if I am being honest, myself. I wanted to examine and if possible conquer my own fears and know what it felt like to touch that curved scimitar-shaped tail, to feel those enlarged, tendon-rippled feet clambering up my arm and whiskers tickling my cheek. I wanted to better understand rat emotion and intelligence, and to find out if there might be a way we could live alongside each other. And I wanted to hold a rat in my hand and feel its soft fur and the pulse of its little heart beating 400 times a minute.

At the time, lockdown puppies were all the rage in Britain, and so when Liz and I wandered into our local pet shop the owner seemed surprised when we asked if she knew of anyone selling rat pups. She turned to a well-thumbed Filofax and confirmed there was in fact a breeder living a few streets away.

I spoke with her on the phone a day or so later. She told me she bred the rats for her son, who has Asperger's syndrome and a particular affinity with the creatures, and had a new litter on the way. And that is how two dumbo rats we named Molly and Ermintrude came into our lives.

They are called dumbo rats because they have been bred with slightly enlarged, circular ears. Molly and Ermintrude's variegated fur is white and grey, a pattern that reminded us both of Holstein Friesian cattle. But like all fancy rats they are still ultimately brown rats, the same wild species you might spot rootling through your bins.

We did the handover at night in the breeder's garage with the rats costing £10 each. Both came with an A4 printed certificate of authenticity bearing a photograph of them as a pup and detailing exactly when they were born. That first night we lay in bed listening to the rats leaping about between the floors of their cage and rearranging their nest to their own liking by tearing up pieces of cardboard and using them to block up the entrance. The noise recalled a memorable description by Ted Hughes in his poem 'Sing The Rat' as 'the house's poltergeist'. Listening as they squeaked and thrashed, rattled the bars and flipped over their bowl, sending food scattering across their cage and on our landing floor, I realised I had crossed an invisible line. We were bound together now, the rats and us.

CHAPTER TWO
Rat Tails

Before collecting Molly and Ermintrude, the breeder instructed me to bring a receptacle in which to carry them home. I turned up with a spring-loaded live trap which I had previously used to catch a wild rat in our garden and later release in a nearby woodland. With this small act of mercy I was in fact breaking the law. Technically it is illegal to release – rather than kill – a wild rat once you have caught it alive. Even if I persuaded myself I was sparing a life, this was perhaps wishful thinking as I could well have unwittingly released the rat into the territory of a rival colony, which they defend to the death.

A cage made of galvanised steel with an impenetrable inner chamber, it was ridiculously over the top. The breeder gave me a baffled look and, I suspect, questioned my ability to care for two pet rats. Fortunately, she took pity on me and offered an open plastic box the rats wouldn't be able to crawl out of, and told me to leave the cage in the boot. It feels slightly embarrassing as I write this now, but I was genuinely afraid of the two small 4-inch (10cm) long rat pups huddled together as we bumped along the road home.

Liz and I had already acquired rather more luxurious lodgings for the rats, which we had set up on our first-floor landing. Their new home was to be a three-tiered cage with a pink plastic igloo-shaped box at the bottom serving as a nest. On a nearby street someone had dumped an unwanted hamster cage on the pavement, so we stripped that for water bottles, which we sterilised. There was a little bowl filled with pet-shop-bought rat food, a rope ladder a friend had given us for a present, and assorted twigs for the rats to gnaw on. The cage was lined with straw, cardboard and paper. Liz had also made a rat hammock out of an old oven glove, and another from a pair of pants, which we suspended from the top of the cage.

As we lifted Molly and Ermintrude out of the travel box and into their new life, it struck me that this was the first time I had ever handled a rat. As my hand closed around Ermintrude's soft pale fur ('champagne'-coloured, according to her breeder's certificate) and her tail curved around my wrist, I felt an involuntary shudder. Liz played with Molly in her hands for a while, but I placed Ermintrude into the cage as quickly as I could. Afterwards I noticed that even in those few seconds together she had deposited a couple of raisin-shaped rat turds in my lap.

The top hatch of the cage was a little loose but seemed secure enough. When I awoke that first morning and walked to the bathroom, I noticed in the corner of my eye a shadow stalking along the skirting and only Ermintrude staring out at me from the cage – Molly had escaped. Eventually we coaxed her out from behind a pot plant, gratified that despite her newfound freedom she hadn't strayed far from her sister and disappeared for good. Once safely back in the cage, I bent the bars so they could not open so easily again and placed a hefty book on top. As we went downstairs for breakfast, the rats slipped into their pink igloo to bed; the nocturnal and diurnal passing briefly by.

It was Charles Darwin who first proposed that disgust served a powerful evolutionary purpose. In 1872, a decade or so after his *Origin of Species* appeared, he published *The Expression of the Emotions in Man and Animals*, which considered the universal emotion of revulsion as something innate, rather than learned. This was, Darwin suggested, developed by our more successful ancestors and passed on through natural selection in order to alert us to health hazards such as spoiled foods.

On one level, he has been proven correct. Disgust (and fear) are undeniably useful tools in keeping us healthy and alive. But there is another – and often equally powerful – sense of moral disgust, which stems from our life experiences, culture and environment. It is this that I believe dictated my feelings towards rats. I'm not sure exactly when, but somewhere along the way I must have been taught to abhor them.

Even the great David Attenborough has previously acknowledged his own fear of rats. 'I really, really hate rats,' he explained in an interview a decade or so ago. 'I don't mean that I mildly dislike them as I dislike, let us say, maggots. I mean that if a rat appears in a room, I have to work hard to prevent myself from jumping on the nearest table.' Ever the naturalist, Attenborough interrogated his own antipathy and boiled it down to the rational (his knowledge of the diseases they can harbour) and irrational (their proximity to humans and lack of fear they display).

It is this tightrope between disgust and fascination along which I wavered in the early days of settling in our two pet rats. Perhaps the feeling was mutual because they also seemed highly suspicious of us and would retreat into their igloo nest whenever we appeared. Slowly, though, we started to coax them out, tapping a seed on the bars and waiting patiently until either Molly or Ermintrude would appear, nose twitching, and snatch it away. Over time they started to take the food directly from our fingers. As they became accustomed to our presence, the rats would also start chattering their teeth. This, I discovered, is called bruxing and a sign of rats relaxing (although they also occasionally do it during periods of heightened stress).

Gradually, we softened towards one another. With each interaction I grew increasingly accustomed to their speed of movement, which seemed to enable them to teleport around their cage, their inquisitive sniffing and licking of my fingertips and the elegant arc of the overlapping scales of their tails. I was also amazed by their hind feet, so human-like with five toes and bare pink flesh. When they would grip our hands to gain better leverage, their front paws were cool to touch with four pointy clawed fingers that dug slightly into the flesh.

Sometimes, though, the rats would push me too far. Such as early on when Molly crawled up my arm and onto my shoulder and I could feel her whiskers tickling my neck and her rat breath on my ear. At this tender and trusting moment, I was forced to call for Liz to help get her off.

Liz, by the way, had no such inner turmoil. She had wanted rats for pets ever since she was young and displayed (to my addled mind at least) sheer courage plunging her hand into the rat cage to tickle them, while I gingerly fed them from behind the bars and winced as they gripped my finger.

Still, I made steady progress through rat therapy. Soon in the long winter lockdown, playing with our rats came to be a daily highlight. At the time I followed a rat enthusiast on Twitter who would periodically tweet at 4 p.m. that this is the best moment of the day, because the rats are waking up.

Touch is my abiding memory of the deprivation of lockdown. I was lucky, of course, to be living with a person I loved when so many others were alone, but even so life was still marked by an absence of human contact. With friends and family reduced to flickering faces on a computer screen, we found solace instead in rats.

As we stroked and tickled Molly and Ermintrude, I was surprised to discover they responded in turn. I had assumed they would be indifferent to affection and at best might merely tolerate the odd caress in return for some food. Instead, once they had established that we were not a threat, they started actively seeking out the feeling of our fingers on their fur.

The rats were also very affectionate towards each other. When not fastidiously washing themselves, they would groom one another, with Ermintrude (the larger and more dominant of the pair) pinning Molly down with her paws. We would often find them squashed into the oven-glove hammock together, sometimes layered in a rat sandwich with their tails drooping out at either end.

In those early days it was not uncommon for them to also engage in spectacular playfights. They would start at the top of the cage and end up rolling down all three floors together, squeaking loudly and kicking up their bedding. During the day they slept together, curled up in a ball in their nest. They would use one corner of the cage as a toilet and when they emerged, sleepily, would perform the most delightful ratty yawns; all the better to display their two pairs of front incisors stained a deep ochre.

Around that time I interviewed neuroscientist Francis McGlone for an article about what lockdown was doing to our brains. McGlone, a professor at Liverpool John Moores University, is an expert investigator into the role of nerve fibres in humans called C-tactile afferents. These are located in parts of the body that are hard to reach, such as the neck and shoulders, and are hard-wired for the pleasure of intimate touch. This means that the act of stroking or hugging stimulates the release of a hormone called oxytocin, which in turn reduces stress and makes us feel good. McGlone admitted he was extremely worried about the mental and physical health impacts of so much of the human population being suddenly deprived of touch.

He had helped develop his theories with some interesting studies on rats. McGlone told me about an academic paper he had recently co-authored, which documented tickling rats to analyse the impact on their behaviour and how it regulated their hormone levels. Their research found that 10 minutes of tickling a day, even when rats were exposed to chronic mild stress such as cat odour, lights and noise, still soothed them and increased their resilience towards the effects of more acute stress. McGlone described this to me

as 'affective touch' and 'the glue that holds us all together';
both humans and rats.

Touch is regarded as our earliest evolutionary language.
Like rats, we would groom one another in what is described
as 'tactile communication' long before we developed speech.
Touch is the first sense a foetus experiences, while studies
have shown it is also the first critical sense a baby develops
to distinguish between self and other.

Caressing a rat is a little like stroking a cat or dog, but on
fast-forward, as this is how they live their lives. We sought to
sit quietly with Molly and Ermintrude, attempting to watch
a film with them huddled on our laps, but this is not the
ratty way. Once out of the cage they would be constantly
exploring, twisting out of our hands and squeezing into the
gaps between our backs and the sofa cushions. To try and
contain them, we made them runs out of piles of books in
our living room with food hidden in the corners, watching
as they leafed through the pages in pursuit of a square of
Shreddies. They sniffed and scratched and sprayed their scent
on the carpet and nibbled the soles of my slippers, and I
started developing a fierce affection for our rats.

In 2019, an interesting study was published in the journal
Science, which shed new light on human–rodent relationships.
The study sought to demonstrate the strength of bonds that
can form between people and rats by playing hide and seek.
The German-based researchers trained rats to hide in
various locations until they were found, and also to seek out
people who had hidden. The rats took quickly to the game,
able to adapt to both roles.

What made this study different is that rats were not
rewarded with food (as I was discovering with Molly and
Ermintrude, you can pretty much get a rat to do anything
for a bite) but instead with social interaction. When

successful, the rats received what the study described as 'playful social interaction'. The rats enjoyed the tickling so much that they were recorded as literally jumping for joy whenever they were discovered in one of the games.

Despite the bonds the rats forged with the researchers, the study ended with the rats being killed. The ethical justification for this was to better study the neural pathways that underpinned their hide-and-seek behaviour. The rats were given an overdose of anaesthetic. More commonly in laboratory settings they are exposed to a rising concentration of carbon dioxide, even though this method has been shown to induce distress and even pain in rats.

We have known since the 1990s that rats laugh; high-pitched ultrasonic giggles inaudible to the human ear. We also know that if tickled by people, rats will giggle more readily and form bonds with whoever is playing with them. Rats are capable of empathy, altruism, regret, and possess impressive powers of memory as well as being able to judge the passage of time. We know this through a host of studies, and yet the vast majority of laboratory rats involved in these studies are killed either during, or immediately after, research.

Generally speaking, rats (and other rodents) remain excluded from the sort of legislative and ethical considerations that cover other animals. In the US – where anything up to an estimated 100 million mice and rats are killed each year – they are not even covered by animal welfare laws, meaning scientists have carte blanche to treat them however they see fit. The US is particularly callous among western countries in its treatment of rats. Indeed, the reason that figure is an estimate is because no official count exists as they are not, legally speaking, considered an animal worthy of protection. Instead, rats are regarded, from a legal perspective at least, as biological mechanisms intended for human experimentation.

Across Europe, EU directives have strengthened protection for animals (including rodents), arguing that they can only be used for research where there is convincing scientific justification. This has led to a marked decline in rats being experimented on in the UK over the past decade. According to the latest figures available at the time of writing, in 2022 2.76 million scientific procedures were carried out on living animals, 1.51 million of which were deemed 'experimental procedures' and 12 per cent of which involved rats. This figure marks the lowest number of procedures carried out in a single year since 2002.

Some biologists and philosophers have drawn comparisons between our modern treatment of rats and the brutal primate experiments of the 1950s and 1960s, which deliberately psychologically damaged animals in order to better understand the human mind. The most notorious of these were conducted by the US psychologist Harry Harlow, who analysed maternal separation in baby rhesus monkeys by removing them from their mothers at birth. Harlow designed two maternal replicas, one made out of wire which distributed milk, and another from soft cloth. The baby monkeys would reach for the physical comfort and warmth over receiving any milk. Harlow also constructed a device he labelled the 'Pit of Despair', a vertical chamber into which monkeys were placed as a more efficient method of quickly inducing depression.

Such experiments on primates rightly provoke outrage today, but are not rats equipped with similarly rich emotional lives? Even rodents that exist in the hermetically sealed chambers of laboratories have been shown to adjust their behaviour to the changing seasons. Exactly how they even know in such a regulated environment is not entirely clear, but perhaps they can smell the briefest hint of the bursting buds and falling leaves drifting in on the sterile air, which stirs some genetic memory of an unknown life outside.

Over the centuries we have deliberately bred rats with high blood pressure and a propensity to develop specific tumours and cardiovascular disease. We have grown a human ear on a laboratory rat's back and grafted the decapitated head of an infant rat onto an adult rat's thigh in order to investigate the impact of blood flow on brain function. We have electrocuted rats, drowned them and trained them to self-administer cocaine and heroin. Rats are sentient creatures that feel pleasure and pain, and yet within a bulk of the scientific community and society at large, anything is deemed acceptable, so long as it benefits us.

We humans like to furnish our own history with stories of heroic hunter-gatherers, but would it surprise you to know that we instead descend from a rat? In 2017, an undergraduate student at Portsmouth University discovered two sets of fossilised teeth in some samples of early Cretaceous rocks gathered on the Dorset coast. The teeth were confirmed as belonging to rat-like creatures that lived 145 million years ago, when dinosaurs still roamed the earth, and are understood to be the earliest direct ancestors of most mammals living today, from the pygmy shrew to humans.

These small mammals were not dissimilar to modern-day rats in both size and behaviour: nocturnal, omnivorous and able to climb and burrow. The early humans who roamed the earth between 2 million and 3 million years ago were also distinctly rat-like in behaviour. In his recent book, *The Meat Paradox*, Rob Percival describes humanity living in the treeline, roaming grasslands where we foraged for food, and with strong arms and curved hands that enabled us to climb. We had developed stone tools to butcher meat (3-million-year-old relics of which have been discovered in Ethiopia) but lacked the wherewithal to hunt larger and more ferocious prey. Instead, we scavenged; waiting and watching for opportunities to arise. Our tools meant we were able to secure nutrients from carcasses left behind by the likes of sabre-tooth tigers. We were, in other words, the prehistoric equivalent of a keen-eyed rat, lurking in the undergrowth for a scrap of kebab meat to fall from another, more lethal predator.

Genetic evidence suggests that around this period (between 2.9 million and 0.9 million years ago), the brown rat diverged from the other Eurasian *Rattus* species (of which there are more than 60 distinct rodents in the genus today). Nowadays the two most common species around the world are the brown rat, *Rattus norvegicus* (the one you will see scuttling about the streets at night), and the black rat, *Rattus rattus*, once common in Britain but now driven to the edge of localised extinction and displaced by their larger and more aggressive cousins, who are better suited to colder northern European climates.

At some undetermined point in their history, both species firmly yoked themselves to human activity and spread across the world from their native homes of the Indian subcontinent, in the case of the black rat, and China, in the case of the brown.

Over millennia rats have followed the rise and fall of empires, their global dispersal offering a detailed map of human history. In 2022, the first ancient genetic study of the black rat was published by researchers at York and Oxford University alongside Germany's Max Planck Institute. The study analysed the remains of black rats at

archaeological sites across Europe spanning the first to
seventeenth centuries. After finding distinct genetic
signatures on rat bones from both the Roman and medieval
periods, the study concluded that the black rat colonised
Europe at least twice.

The rats arrived with the Romans and perhaps even
disappeared with the collapse of their empire, the researchers
argued, only to return when long-range international trade
resumed during the medieval period. Backing up this theory,
the study discovered the Roman rat skeletons from England
to eastern Europe formed a single group in genetic terms
and one entirely distinct from the later medieval rat bones
(which also formed their own distinct group). Dr David
Orton, one of the archaeologists involved, said at the time
that the research team 'couldn't have hoped for clearer
evidence of repeated colonisation of Europe'.

Brown rats are a more recent arrival from the east, but
nobody seems sure exactly when. Originally adapted to the
colder climes of northern China and Mongolia, certainly it
is now assumed that brown rats arrived in Europe well
before the eighteenth century (when it is still often
commonly claimed they first appeared). Rat skeletons are
notoriously difficult for archaeologists to assess as subsequent
generations of rodents will also often burrow underground,
disturbing other finds and disrupting history. Various studies
in Germany, however, have discovered the remains of what
are thought to be contemporary brown rats in former
medieval settlements, including the village of Klein Freden,
near Salzgitter, which was occupied between the ninth and
thirteenth centuries.

The British army officer and doctor William Porter
MacArthur was one of the first to challenge the prevailing
orthodoxy about when rats arrived in the west. MacArthur,

who had served on the Western Front during the First World War and in his later medical research developed a particular interest in plague and other tropical diseases, disputed what was then a broad scientific consensus that black rats had arrived in the west with the return of the Crusaders around the twelfth century Instead, he argued, these rats were commonplace to the Romans and responsible for being the carriers of the Justinian Plague of the sixth century (named after the Byzantine emperor Justinian I and known as the first Old World plague pandemic).

Previously, medical historians had questioned how such a plague could have come about with no rats in the western world to bear the fleas, but MacArthur argued they were in fact commonplace across Roman Europe. To back up his then explosive claims, he cited various archaeological finds, including an Etruscan tablet showing a rat gnawing on a ship's rope and the discovery of rat skeletons in the ashes of Pompeii.

In her seminal work *Les Chemins de la Peste*, the French archaeologist and historian Frédérique Audoin-Rouzeau mentions various studies developing MacArthur's work in the latter half of the twentieth century, which confirmed the presence of rats on European soil from Roman times at least. In particular, she cites the discovery of black rat bones along major maritime and trade routes used by the empire, including London, York and the great Roman road stretching south to north across England.

Outside of her work in archaeology and plague history, Audoin-Rouzeau moonlights as a wildly successful author of Parisian crime dramas under the pseudonym Fred Vargas. One of her books envisages an attempt to unleash a modern-day Black Death upon the city by killers who keep rats and cultivate their fleas. Its title, *Have Mercy on Us*

All, borrows the words daubed onto the front door of London plague victims alongside a red cross which Samuel Pepys noted in his diaries of the summer of 1665: 'Lord, Have Mercy Upon Us.'

Our long-standing companionship with rats has led to a rich seam in British folklore. Rat-like creatures shape and scuttle through our stories. In Scottish folklore there is the lavellan, a rodent-like critter based on the rat, or perhaps a water shrew, whose mildly toxic bite is poisonous enough to immobilise some amphibians and small fish. In his seventeenth-century text *Scotia Illustrata*, the Scottish natural historian Robert Sibbald described the lavellan as 'an animal common in Caithness, it stays in water, it has a head similar to the weasel, and is a beast of the same colouring. The breath from these beasts does harm'.

In some more outlandish tales, the lavellan's breath was claimed to be so venomous that it could poison livestock from 40 yards away. 'Let him not go away from the houses, to moss or wood, lest the Lavellan come and smite him,' said one satirical song of the time.

During the witch trials of the sixteenth and seventeenth centuries, rats were regarded as familiars of the devil. In *Macbeth*, one of the witches promises to turn herself into a rat to pursue a sailor overseas. 'And, like a rat without a tail,' she warns, 'I'll do, I'll do and I'll do'.

Rats feature prominently in modern stories. Every few weeks or so, seemingly another rat story appears in the newspapers. At the time of writing, so many rats have apparently taken up residence in the nineteenth-century Palace of Westminster that cats are no longer allowed on the parliamentary estate for fear they will consume one of the many poison traps laid down in an attempt to kill the rodents. Meanwhile, thousands of residents living in Hertfordshire recently lost all internet access after rats chewed their way through heavy duty broadband cables, which are normally so tough they require a drill to get through.

There are also more fantastical tales. One told in cities all over the world is of the fabled 'rat king', whereby so many rodents cluster together that their tails entwine and become one swirling mass. While some photographs exist online, many experts believe this is myth. Other urban legends, such as the Rat-man of Southend, tell the story of the faceless ghost of a homeless man who was eaten alive by rats, haunting a city underpass.

In their native far-east, rats are viewed with far more appreciation than the lands they have invaded. The rat is the first sign of the Chinese Zodiac, indicating charm, intelligence and gregariousness. In Japan, rats appeared widely in historic artworks as symbols of familial prosperity and social success. In one surviving early seventeenth-century Japanese manual of mathematics, children were even taught geometry using symbols of rats. And in India, the elephant god Ganesha travels the world on a rat to help remove any obstacle in his path.

Contrast that to western childhoods where a loathing of rats is drilled into us and violence towards them excused. Rifling through the library one day I came across a children's rhyme from the 1870s in a book entitled *Rambling Rhymes for Little Ones*. It goes:

An old woman troubled with rats,
Who couldn't depend upon cats — [...]
Had a fine large extinguisher made,

Then in her barn quietly laid; —
'I'll catch all the tyrants,' she said.
At the very first sight of a rat,
She popped the extinguisher pat,
Which caught him as well as a cat.
And so she went on every day,
Till she frightened the rats all away.

One of my favourite quotes about rats comes from the graffiti artist Banksy, who has painted them throughout his career. He was in turn inspired by the Parisian artist Blek le Rat, who in the early 1980s made his name stencilling rodent depictions on the streets of the city. Blek le Rat described his muse as 'the only free animal living in the city'. Banksy, meanwhile, who during the first lockdown in 2020 sneaked onto a Circle Line tube train to spray images of rats sneezing and parachuting using face masks, celebrates the urban rat because they 'exist without permission'.

That speaks to me of a counterpoint to the desire in western culture for nature to be submissive or subservient to human needs. Perhaps this also explains why our own rat stories are largely imbued with a sense of destruction. Rats are wildlife in the truest sense. Wilder, in fact, because they thrive in spite of human interventions to control their populations. They are nature's anarchists, subverting and challenging our own carefully constructed hierarchies. 'Rats!' wrote Robert Browning in his 1842 poem 'The Pied Piper of Hamelin'. 'They fought the dogs, and killed the cats/And bit the babies in the cradles/And eat the cheeses out of the vats.'

A few months after Molly and Ermintrude settled in and lockdown restrictions had eased, I boarded a train for the

German town of Hamelin, made famous by rats. Every Sunday lunchtime in the summer months the town hosts a free open-air performance of the Pied Piper legend and I wanted to see the origins of perhaps the best-known rat story of all.

Hamelin in summer is a frenzy of rat tourism. The high streets are filled with gift shops selling rat fridge magnets, T-shirts and mugs. Bakeries display hard-baked decorative rat-shaped pastries with straw whiskers. Visitors follow walking routes indicated by bronze rats embossed on the pavements and the image of the Pied Piper adorns everything from the stained-glass window of the main church to the green man at traffic lights.

I arrive a few minutes before the noon performance. The wooden benches in the main square are already crowded with tourists from around the world sitting in the beating heat. I sit in front of a Dutch couple, who offer me some sun cream. The rows ahead are filled with Chinese tourists in socks and sandals.

After the church chimes sound, the Pied Piper appears, resplendent in orange and yellow tights, shoes with long curled tips and a feather plume in his hat. He plays a clarinet as he leads a procession of a dozen or so children dressed up as rats onto the stage. In my youth my grandmother occasionally requisitioned my brother and me to appear wearing tights and brandishing a shield in the medieval fair parade of Boston, Lincolnshire, where she lived. I assume for the young people of Hamelin today, dressing up as a rat is a similar rite of passage that must be observed.

The play is set against a backdrop of medieval Hamelin painted on a canvas sheet that flaps faintly in the weak breeze. The story is similar to the version Robert Browning told, and which has persisted since medieval times. The Pied Piper is

recruited by the townsfolk to rid them of rats and manages to
lure them into drowning in the river Weser by hypnotising
them with his magical tune. However, after killing the rats, he
is refused payment by the leaders of the town. And so in a
revenge parable for the ages about always paying your dues,
the Pied Piper summons the children of Hamelin and leads
them away into the mountains, never to return.

An inscription on the so-called Pied Piper's house in the
centre of Hamelin records this as a true historical event. It
reads: 'A.D. 1284 – on the 26th of June – the day of St John
and St Paul – 130 children – born in Hamelin – were led
out of the town by a piper wearing multicoloured clothes.
After passing the Calvary near the Koppenberg they
disappeared forever.' Meanwhile an entry in the town
records, apparently dating to 1384, claims sorrowfully, 'It is
100 years since our children left'.

The Hamelin Museum is filled with variations of the
Pied Piper story and others it has inspired over the centuries.
Ibsen's late-nineteenth-century play *Little Eyolf*, for example,
features an enchantress called the Rat-Wife able to coax out
rodents and drown them in a fjord. The museum posits
various theories for the origins of the Pied Piper story, one
of the most convincing of which is that the children left as
part of a widespread eastern migration of Germans to settle
rapidly expanding frontiers. The pipers were in reality
recruiters, aiming to drum up potential settlers and lead
them away in search of a new life.

While visiting Hamelin, rat stories started burrowing into
my brain. At the time, I was also reading *The Rat* by the
twentieth-century German author Günter Grass. The book
begins with Grass's narrator receiving a caged female rat for
Christmas, a gift which sparks a long and rambling history
of the world from a rat's perspective. The 'She-rat', as Grass

calls her, talks to him in his dreams and outlines a dystopian future in which humans have destroyed themselves with nuclear weapons and the rats are in charge.

Around the time Grass was writing his book, it was known that rats living on the Marshall Islands in the Pacific Ocean had survived the nuclear tests conducted there following the Second World War. In 1998, a team of Russian researchers studying the radiation resistance of various animals discovered that rats did have significantly higher survival rates than any other species. This hardiness is in part down to rats' natural – and remarkable – tolerance to hypoxia (a potentially fatal condition caused by low oxygen levels in body tissue).

While the rat may indeed outlast us, our histories are inextricably interwoven. Witnessing so many fellow rat tourists in Hamelin who had travelled from all over the world, strengthened this notion of a shared past between people and rats. At one point Günter Grass's narrator muses: 'Is the rat even conceivable without man?' The reverse could also be argued. Rats have always been there, and yet we continue to regard them as interlopers into our world.

You will find scant mention of rats in the Bible, just a vague reference in Leviticus 11:29 to 'creeping things that creep upon this earth'. Isaiah 66:17 cautions that anyone who consumes mouse (then an interchangeable word for rat), swine and other unclean beings will meet a terrible end. Matthew 6:19 urges worshippers not to store up their treasures on earth 'where moths and vermin destroy' but instead store them up for heaven where rats, presumably, are barred at the gates.

A few modern books have attempted to redress this. Jonathan Burt's aforementioned *Rat* published nearly 20 years ago offers an excellent overview of the rodent's place in cultural history. More recently, Lisa T. Sarasohn's history of vermin, *Getting Under Our Skin*, provides a wealth of rat stories. Sarasohn's book is mainly preoccupied with lice, bedbugs and fleas, although she admits rats nosed their way into a few chapters.

Both books, however, analyse the rat primarily from a human perspective. There is indeed plenty of merit in learning more about ourselves from rats. As Sarasohn writes, 'More than any other vermin, people see themselves in rats, which have been inescapable figures in the human landscape'. But I also hoped to better understand rats as a species on their own terms. Rather than viewed purely through the prism of human fascination and loathing, I wished to explore their hidden world. To see rats as rats, rather than vermin or pests. I now had a pair of She-rats, chattering in their cage back at home, to assist.

CHAPTER THREE

Tunnels

Beneath my home city of Sheffield is a shadowland, a place of narrow stone tunnels and subterranean vaults of palatial scale. Over the years living here I have seen glimpses of this other world, occasionally peering into the yawning gape of storm drains or beneath the arches of road bridges and wondering what secrets they concealed.

The thought of ever venturing below prompted a claustrophobic shudder, although I knew, like a condemned man, that when I started writing this book it would ultimately lead me down towards this unfamiliar world and into the domain of the rats. While I could learn much about both rat and human relationships from Molly and Ermintrude, I also needed to seek out colonies in the wild that exist in a daily struggle for survival. And where better to encounter a rat, than in the bowels of a city?

It is towards this hidden world that I am crawling now, stooping low under a Victorian brick-built tunnel illuminated in the weak light of my headtorch. My rucksack scrapes on the narrowing ceiling gradually closing around me. I measure my breaths against waves of rising panic. At 6 foot 2ins I am suited for life above ground. The great physical prowess of rats is to compress and squeeze their skeletal frames through holes of ever-diminishing size, but such a prospect is one of my greatest fears.

The space I am in keeps shrinking as I struggle through. For the last 50 metres or so before reaching the pinprick of light at the end of the passageway, I am forced to scrabble through the darkness, lumbering in a rat-like crawl. I emerge into daylight by Sheffield train station and a 100-metre or so stretch of riverbank in the open air. After even this briefest of spells underground, my senses are greedily heightened to the world above: the purple horns of swaying buddleia, the diesel engines idling at the nearby station cab rank and the sickly smell of Himalayan balsam.

A last breath of the sweet, familiar city and then another tunnel plunges me once more into darkness. This time I find myself in an arched labyrinth where the river Sheaf meets the Porter Brook underground. This section of river was covered over in the mid nineteenth century during the construction of the train station and has remained so ever since. Over the sound of the flowing rivers, I can hear the screeching trains pull in at platform 5, located somewhere directly above my head through half a metre of brick and rubble.

My journey into the darkness is the culmination of a rat-scoping exercise that started several years previously along Sheffield's river Sheaf in a park just outside the city centre, where I would often take a walk during lockdown. From a footbridge I would watch grey wagtails flitting over stones in the shimmering shallows, moorhens and a lone mandarin duck. But my favourite sighting was always one of the rats in the colony that lived along the riverbank.

I watched them dart furtively out from the undergrowth to forage for whatever treat might have washed up. Rivers provide rich feeding grounds for omnivore rats. Observers elsewhere in the country have even recorded rats diving several feet down to retrieve freshwater mussels. This astonishing behaviour trait has been reported on the river Nene in Cambridgeshire, the Norfolk Broads and Somerset Levels. During those lockdown days the best thing I ever saw them snaffle was a few discarded chips.

The Sheaf is the river from which Sheffield takes its name, an ancient border marker between the old Anglo-Saxon kingdoms of Mercia and Northumbria, formed by a series of gritstone streams about 6 miles south-west from the city centre on the edge of the Peak District. From there the river flows alongside the Midland rail line into the centre of Sheffield, where it disappears in an extensive network of underground culverts before flowing into the river Don.

The Sheaf is also where the modern-day city started. Sheffield Castle was constructed in the early twelfth century at the spot where the Sheaf flows into the Don, and a growing population slowly spread along its banks. As industry boomed, lead smelting, paper and corn mills and steel forging, rolling, grinding and finishing works proliferated along the river and its waters became rapidly despoiled.

By the nineteenth century, the Sheaf was regarded as little more than an open sewer, a source of the cholera epidemics that ravaged the slums of the Steel City and a breeding ground for malarial mosquitos. When permission was granted to begin construction of the new Midland railway to London in the 1860s, the river was buried. Huge stone arches provided supports for the station above. The Sheaf was abandoned to course silently through the darkness; a river of the underworld.

Nowadays, the Sheaf and Porter Rivers Trust (a community organisation working to reveal Sheffield's lost rivers) occasionally organises guided tours of the culverts. Our guide points out fragments of oyster shells eaten by the labourers who helped construct the station, broken grindstones, and the remains of old clay crucibles used in the steel-making process. Trudging through this Stygian realm, I catch glimpses of the ghosts of the former city all around. I am reminded of Robert Macfarlane's book *Underland*, in which he spends several days exploring the catacombs of Paris. Macfarlane cites Italo Calvino's novel *Invisible Cities*, where the narrator describes the city of Eusapia, mirrored by an identical copy underground.

My headtorch illuminates the skeletal glow of a crayfish cruising through the underground river while spiderwebs shimmer above. We walk further along into a vast underground culvert, known locally as the Megatron, where the Sheaf makes its final journey before tipping into the Don. At the far end is a roosting colony of Daubenton's bats, which we keep well clear of to avoid disturbing. The bats thrive on the underground river and its healthy population of caddisflies and midges, using their tails and feet to scoop up the insects from the water.

What of rats, I ask our guide? I came down here expecting to find them scuttling and squeaking over our feet. Yet over the course of the underground tour I have not spotted a single one, nor indeed any evidence of rat activity. It is a question, he tells me, they are regularly asked. Some people join these walking tours to confront their own musophobia (an irrational and overwhelming fear of rodents), others in the hope of a rat safari. But in the many dozens of times he has stalked these underground caverns, the guide says, he has never encountered a single rat. Possibly seeing the disappointment on my face through the gloom, he adds: 'But I'm sure they are down here.'

The Sheaf runs a few hundred metres from my home, and I have watched the river in all weathers. Narrow and fast-flowing as it courses through local parks, on summer days children play in its shallows. In periods of prolonged rainfall, however, the river swells into a muddy roar. Its waters can turn an opaque orange as the abandoned mines along its tributaries boil over. During the Sheffield floods of 2007, a 14-year-old boy was swept to his death after accidentally falling in.

While life along the river Sheaf became strangled by noxious gas, heavy metals and chemicals during the Industrial Revolution, over recent decades it has gradually recovered. An increase in invertebrate activity has resulted in birds and fish, including wild brown trout, returning to its waters, although like all urban rivers in the modern era it continues to suffer from chronic sewage outflows and chemical pollution.

The neglected state of many urban rivers like the Sheaf, the rubbish that is dumped there and the proximity to businesses and homes, all make them an ideal habitat for rats to construct their burrows. While spending most of their time out of water, rats are supremely adept swimmers and capable of holding their breath for long periods of time. One *National Geographic* experiment in 2015 demonstrated the ease at which a rat can swim up a toilet pipe, navigating its turns in a matter of seconds by twisting its body and paddling with its claws. It is said that rats can swim through water currents of up to 30mph.

The culverted sections of the Sheaf and Porter Brook, I presumed, would offer an even better habitat for rats, away from other predators such as herons, foxes and birds of prey that stalk the open stretches of riverbank. And so I set my sights downstream. My idea was to follow the river in order to take a rat's eye view of the city, and to explore the hidden corners it might reveal.

We tend to think of cities entirely in anthropogenic terms, places where humans congregate and nature might occasionally flourish if we somehow permit it. But such a view dismisses the life that exists in parallel to our own. In 2022, a small-budget Indian documentary called *All That Breathes* explored this theme through the story of two brothers who set up an animal hospital in a basement in Delhi, rescuing the black kites that feed on the city's rubbish dumps. The film was heralded at international festivals and ultimately nominated for an Oscar, but above all it is a celebration of municipal scavengers, the overlooked and occasionally maligned creatures regarded as pests. There are lingering, beautifully constructed shots of rats feeding, mosquitos hatching in puddles and snails slowly gliding over a wall.

When the film was shown at the London Film Festival, I was commissioned to interview the director, Shaunak Sen, for a newspaper article. As we sat down at a table at a swanky hotel in Mayfair, chosen by the festival publicity team, we quickly realised our shared interest in unfashionable species; the sort that would shut such an establishment down if ever spotted inside. Shaunak told me his aim was to ensure the film was not just a story of 'good people doing good things' but something that spoke more widely about urban ecosystems. 'The idea was to zoom out and make people contemplate on the bigger thing of urban ecology and life writ large upon the canvas of the city,' he said. 'Human and non-human life constantly jostling cheek by jowl.'

We spoke at length about rats. The film's opening shot is several minutes of unbroken footage of a large colony of rats in a crowded residential area of Old Delhi. Unlike so much other filming of rats, often overblown and distorted to instil fear in the viewer, he shows them as they are, explorative, inquisitive, working individually but as a collective. Shaunak spent two nights ensuring he secured the right shots. As the film crew worked, he told me, the rats would run over their feet and jump up on their shoes. 'We were getting used to them and they were getting used to us,' he said.

According to Shaunak Sen, such is the multitude of overlapping religious beliefs in India that it is difficult to summarise how people generally feel about rats. At the famous Rat Temple of Karni Mata in Rajasthan, for example, devotees worship the Hindu saint and goddess, and regard rats as representatives both of her living form and the lives of their ancestors. There are tens of thousands of rats scurrying about the temple, which are cared for by local priests. The worshippers at the temple believe that when a person dies, they are reborn a rat. When a rat dies, it is reincarnated in human form. The rats are given bowls of milk to drink from and left piles of food as offerings.

While some deify the rodents, others regard them as pests to be exterminated. Certainly though, he says, there is less of the animosity present in much of western culture, and a greater sense of empathy towards the lives they are trying to eke out among all the other inhabitants of the city. When it rains in Delhi and their burrows are flooded, he says, there is a sort of rat amnesty declared for the rodents scurrying to find new homes. People will not kill them when they are clearly desperate and in need.

One of Shaunak Sen's great inspirations is Maan Barua, a lecturer in human geography at Cambridge University who focuses in particular on urban ecologies and novel ways of understanding the flow of the city. I am particularly intrigued by his work on how non-human life utilises infrastructure to its own ends. Barua describes termites burrowing into building timbers, macaques causing power outages in India by swinging from electricity pylons instead of forest vines and, of course, the greatest stowaway of them all, the rat, which hitches a lift on the global cargo-carrying fleet to explore nearly every corner of the world.

Barua argues that 'infrastructures have become a vital thread in understanding the intensity and scale of other-than-human movement'. The canalised and culverted stretches of the river Sheaf where it meets the city centre force the river into a form entirely by human design. An infrastructure, therefore, that is ideal for rats to exploit.

Every city possesses these underground portals to another world. In 2020, one appeared in New York, swallowing a person into the shadows. It was big news at the time and I remember reading about it with horror. A 33-year-old man called Leonard Shoulders was strolling past a bus stop in the Bronx when a sinkhole opened up in the pavement and he disappeared inside. Mr Shoulders was trapped in a chasm 15 feet (4.5 metres) deep for around 30 minutes before rescuers could free him from the debris. He suffered various minor injuries to his arms and legs but the worst of his 'nightmare' ordeal, he later recounted, was the rats. As he lay in the darkness he felt rats crawling all over him and was even afraid to cry for help for fear a rat would climb into his mouth.

It is a story that speaks to a shared fear of the invisible city felt by many urban inhabitants. That beneath our feet, a legion of rats lurks in wait. My journey into Sheffield's subterranean rivers, however, and conversations with those spending considerable time underground had started to offer a very different perspective of rodent populations. They are far more dispersed than we might imagine.

Richard Ashley is one of the few researchers to interrogate this. An emeritus professor of urban water at Sheffield University, he has spent much of his career working on, and in, sewers. He started in London in the 1970s as a draughtsman surveying the city's sewage outflows at a time when much of the Victorian-built system was not fully mapped. Back then, he says, the sewermen (as they nearly all were) would often gleefully swap grisly tales of rats but rarely encountered one. Indeed, the original nickname for the labourers who constructed London's sewer network was 'sewer rats'. One well-told story in the tunnels, Ashley says, was that if you met a rat head-on in a tunnel it would aggressively launch itself at your face. But, as he points out in defence, the rats are just trying to escape through the gap between your head and shoulder.

Around the 1980s, he started conducting research on where and how rats lived in the sewer system, in order to analyse the best means of controlling populations. It was an era when local authorities were employed in constant baiting of rats in sewers with poison, a practice Ashley quickly concluded was a waste of time. To aid his work, he enlisted the help of a specialist pest-controller, David Channon, and together the pair constructed a copy of the sewer system in a garage, complete with a network of branches and manholes. A dozen wild rats were then captured in London and released into the model sewer, which was equipped with infrared cameras to monitor their every move.

The rats, Ashley recalls, quickly formed a colony and would cluster together under the manhole nearest to where food was released into the system. However, they noticed that for some reason a couple of rats were ostracised from the main group and retreated to live in the furthest corner of the sewer. One ended up with its head bitten off, the other escaped. The rest of the rats stayed together in a happy unit, sleeping in a pile during the day and sharing the resources they were given.

David Channon later took the experiment further and ultimately published a PhD on a 13-year study of monitoring sewers in Enfield, north London. His study indicated an overall reduction in rat activity over the period from 1986 to 1999. Channon carried on this work until the Covid lockdown, when he deemed the variables had become too great due to both shifts in human activity, such as people working from home, and climate change altering the weather patterns.

Again, the chief conclusion of his work was that there are far fewer rats in the sewers than we have been led to believe.

At the highest count, the researchers detected evidence of rodents in around 20 per cent of the manholes. At its lowest, this was close to zero. 'There is certainly a lot less rat activity than popular perception,' the 72-year-old tells me over the phone one day from Devon, where he now lives. 'Many of the public think the sewers are occupied by rats all the time, which is wrong.'

Channon became involved in the pest-control industry around 40 years ago almost by accident. After finishing a psychology degree at university he established a bee-keeping business but kept being called out to attend reported honeybee swarms that were in fact wasp nests. He started charging to remove the nests, and then dealing with rats became a natural next step. 'Extremely intelligent animals,' he tells me. 'We certainly won't be killing them off with any kinds of poisons.'

Channon's business took a different approach to many in the pest-control industry, hiring trained biologists to analyse rat behaviour and develop preventative tools. He decided to eschew poisons wherever possible and instead focus on educating customers about better managing their waste and rat-proofing buildings to deter infestations. 'We have spent more of our recorded history trying to kill rats than almost any other pest, with only ever short-term success,' he tells me.

Channon points out that whatever weapon we have deployed in our arsenal, rats have always remained one step ahead. When we first used acute poisons such as arsenic, the neophobic rats quickly developed avoidance behaviour. When we countered that with chronic anticoagulants to slowly poison them, they developed a stronger tolerance by becoming resistant to the chemicals and also helped each other to avoid suspicious substances through both the smell of faeces of other rats and even cues passed on in their mother's milk.

Over time, he has concluded that the rat population is far smaller, more dispersed and less of an issue than the pest-control industry has led us to believe. 'A lot of their marketing is fear marketing,' he says. 'The actual numbers they put out and size of rats they show pictures of are generally exaggerated. I can't blame them for it. It's a tough world and marketing is marketing, whatever you are selling.'

Channon has dug into the oft-quoted statistic of there being one rat for every person in Britain and attributes it to an Edwardian scientist called W. R. Boelter. After examining reports from farmers, landowners and estate agents, Boelter concluded that there was a population density of around one rat per cultivated acre. There were around 40 million acres in cultivation across the UK at the time and the population was roughly the same amount. Whether or not the evidence upon which this original assumption was made was sound, over the subsequent century, as Channon points out, while the UK population has risen to 67 million there has been a decline in the area of cultivated land. One of the best overviews of the current rat population, he argues, was conducted in 1995 and published in *A Review of British Mammals*, in which researchers estimated the UK rat population to be as low as 6.75 million.

Over the years, Channon has recorded detailed footage of rats in sewer networks and helped construct an interesting picture of the daily life of a rat. According to his research, 49 per cent of their time is spent sleeping (mostly in dry locations), 29 per cent feeding, 16 per cent gnawing and 5 per cent grooming.

He has filmed rats crouching in pipes above the flow of sewage in the pitch black, using their sense of smell to pick out grains and tomato seeds from the torrent of human waste. He has also witnessed the agility and ingenuity of rats as they swim through sewage pipes against strong currents of water. And he has observed the close bonds that form within colonies.

We think of rats leading savage, individualistic lives, but a breadth of studies have confirmed that they possess an ingrained sense of altruism when it comes to helping out their own. In 2011, a well-known University of Illinois experiment demonstrated that if a rat becomes trapped in a plastic tube, a fellow, unrestrained rat will operate a latch until it works out how to free its stricken cage mate. Over the course of the 12-day experiment it took the rat five days to learn how to fully operate the latch mechanism. By the final day, it could expertly release the latch in a matter of seconds to set its fellow rat free.

In 2015, scientists in Japan developed an experiment to investigate this further. They designed a partitioned box with a transparent screen, separating a tank of water and a dry platform, with a button that opened the divide. Two rats were then placed in the box for up to 300 seconds at a time, one in the water and one on the dry side. The rat in the pool was not at risk of drowning because it could cling to a ledge, but would still have to tread water unless its fellow rat pressed the button to open the partition between them.

After repeating the experiment with different pairs of rats over several days, the researchers found the dry rats would regularly aid those trapped in the water by opening the door. However, when they shared the box with no water in, they were far less likely to operate the button to lift the divide. This, the team of scientists concluded, demonstrated that rats were not merely rescuing each other out of companionship but through a genuine sense of empathy with those who were struggling. The researchers introduced one final curveball into the experiment, placing the temptation of chocolate cereal for the dry rat on the platform, with the option that it could either eat that, or rescue the rat in the pool. The rodents chose to help their companions above going for the chocolate between 50 and 80 per cent of the time.

There is now a growing field of neuroscience that suggests rats are hard-wired to prioritise and rescue their closest companions in times of crisis (just as is the case with humans). In recent years, a research team at University of California, Berkeley, has been working to identify the brain networks in rats that respond to empathy and whether they are mirrored in humans. Using a range of diagnostic tools to monitor the neural pathways in rats as they respond to trapped companions, they concluded that they react in much the same way as people – registering an emotional reaction to any rat in distress, but being far more likely to leap into action when it is a companion they recognise.

Rats also remember their own adverse experiences, and this is perhaps why they often prefer a life above ground. As David Channon points out, life in the sewers is becoming increasingly dangerous as we experience unprecedented rainfall patterns at unpredictable times of year. Flash-flooding means Britain's sewers are often now pushed beyond their capacity and fill up entirely with water (hence the readiness of water companies to open up sewage outflows into rivers). While adult rats could swim to safety, their hairless pups would not be able to cope.

I think back to popular folk-horror descriptions of an army of rats waiting to rise up from the sewers, then to what these studies and the work of the likes of David Channon and Richard Ashley actually demonstrate. In contrast to the hackneyed and overblown tales of the underground, rats appear to live in colonies far more scattered and tight-knit than we might imagine. There are around 6,000 manholes in the borough of Enfield, David Channon says. Prise one open and peer into the darkness and chances are you would see nothing staring back but your own fears.

My river Sheaf expedition in pursuit of rats had by this stage led me back into the daylight. If rats were not to be found in any significant number in the Megatron or any other of the city-centre river culverts then, I was beginning to conclude, they might be lurking far closer to us. As I researched more of the history of the river and its role in the foundation of Sheffield, I homed in on one final and obvious location: the site of the former Sheffield Castle itself, at the very end of the Sheaf where it forms a confluence with the river Don. After all, this is the heart of ancient Sheffield and the place where the city's inhabitants have lived throughout its history. And where there are people, rats will inevitably follow.

A 2019 study published in the journal *Frontiers in Ecology and Evolution* aimed to pull together the academic literature around urban rat activity to provide a definitive view of how they navigate a city. With the global urban human population set to rise from 55 per cent to 68 per cent by

2050, the study authors argued, it was vital to understand better the spaces we share with rats.

The availability of local food resources, the study concluded, was crucial to where rats choose to live, and the closer the better. On average Norway rats will restrict their movements to between 10 and 20 metres between food and nesting sites, although they are prepared to venture much further if necessary. Norway rats have been recorded dispersing up to 11.5 kilometres to seek out new territories and feeding locations. The study also found rats were happy to exploit human infrastructure, using roads and in particular alleyways, to suit their own ends.

The overall conclusion is that rats prefer us as immediate neighbours. Instead of populations being permanently embedded in sewer systems, rat colonies are far more likely to flit between underground and overground when opportunities arise. That makes controlling them futile unless wider changes to whatever attracted rats in the first place are also enacted. Indeed, the study found that following an 88 per cent reduction in rodents in a location, the population will subsequently increase between 3 and 20 per cent per week as new rats fill the vacuum. Within as little as four weeks following any control measures, rat populations can rebound to more or less what they were before.

A separate study published in 2017 examined 15 years of data between 1996 and 2010, assessing the prevalence of rats and mice around homes in England. This found a higher proportion of rats in older properties and those with drainage faults or outdoor animals housed nearby, and also that socio-economic factors were linked to rodent activity. Deprived areas with more derelict buildings, litter and neglected gardens also recorded significantly higher

numbers of rats. Like creeping mould or high levels of
antisocial behaviour, the rodents reflect the failings of
society back at us.

In a thoughtful article considering rats as part of the
wider urban ecosystem, Canadian public health researcher
Chelsea Himsworth recently argued that rat-related issues
should be treated as a result of policy failure. Rather than
wasting time attempting to eradicate rats, city leaders should
focus attention on the deprived inner-city neighbourhoods
that are disproportionately impacted. Better waste collection,
tougher rules on littering, greater community cohesion and
reducing antisocial behaviour can all help reduce rat activity
without the need to bait a single trap. 'This does not mean
that we should love rats, nor does it mean that we need to
leave them alone,' she writes. 'Rather, it shifts the focus to
managing the ecosystem of which rats are a part, rather than
focusing on the rats themselves.'

After centuries of largely futile efforts to rid cities of
rats, adopting a more benign approach is beginning to gain
currency. One intriguing anthropological study recently
conducted in Amsterdam, considered the rights of rats to
belong in a city. Launched in response to a spate of rat
sightings in and around the Dutch capital and based upon
a wide range of interviews focused on people's daily
interactions with rats, the researchers proposed Amsterdam's
rodents be considered as denizens of the city rather than
invaders. Their burrowing, gnawing, rat runs and
encounters with humans can all be understood as 'acts of
denizenship', the study argues, staking their own claims on
the built environment.

If left alone, and with access to food, urban rat populations
will remain entrenched in the same locations for many
generations, if not centuries. A recent archaeological survey

of the ruins of Sheffield Castle (demolished during the English Civil War in 1646 as a royalist stronghold) found among the fragments of medieval pottery and floor tiles and the bones of livestock slaughtered on site, the remains of several black rats.

Those rats were in all likelihood residents of the slaughterhouses and market stalls that for 700 years filled the streets surrounding the castle. In 1296, Edward I granted a charter to the Lord of the Manor of Sheffield, Thomas de Furnival, permitting a weekly Tuesday market to be held near the site and a three-day fair once a year. From then until the closure of Sheffield's castle market in 2013, the location was the centre of urban food trade – and a rat bazaar.

One writer in 1861 described the scene at the riverside slaughterhouses erected alongside the Don and Sheaf, where carcasses and any cuts of meat that could not be sold were dumped into the water at the end of each working day. The article, from *The Builder* (a nineteenth-century architectural journal, which often carried harrowing reports from northern industrial cities intended to shock more genteel audiences), labelled the area around Castlegate 'a district of slaughter sheds for nearly the whole of Sheffield', where the stench of tripe boiling houses hung over excrement flushed from the tenements above and the 'gory slime' of livestock carcasses. The author described how 'pail-fulls of blood soak down on the surface of the ground and into it through the wretched paving and percolate from slaughter house to slaughter house until the blood oozingly finds its way – together with faecal matter into the river'.

Outside of trading hours, the streets around the area were some of the city's most prominent nightspots, roaring with drunks, music halls, prize fights and betting rings. Several nearby pubs housed their own rat pits in which a dog was released and people would place bets on how many rodents it could kill. One large rat pit at the Blue Bell Inn on Silver Street was operated by a local character called Fagey Joe, who boasted that his pitbull, Bullet, once killed 200 rats in 13 minutes. The landlord of another pub, the Clown and Monkey on Paradise Square, ended up in court accused by a neighbour of deliberately encouraging rats to breed in his basement to ensure a steady supply, leading to the nearby cellars being overrun. Sometimes the bets would take place in the open air in the marketplace itself, with bystanders cheering on the dogs as they mauled whichever rats they could hunt between the stalls.

Once the insalubrious centre of life in Sheffield, ever since I moved here in 2017, Castlegate has stood empty. By then the market had moved to a new indoor location on the other side of the city centre and the old stalls had been demolished. It is a part of the city that has suffered in recent years with shops closing and stalled redevelopment, the formerly bustling marketplace left to the rats who still feed on the takeaway bins nearby. But in late 2021 the council secured £20 million to transform the derelict site, deculverting part of the river Sheaf where it flowed under the old marketplace and excavating the remaining fragments of castle ruins as part of a new riverside park.

In the winter, shortly before the construction work was due to commence, I meet with Simon Ogden, chair of the Sheaf and Porter Rivers Trust, for a tour of the site. Simon was formerly head of urban regeneration at Sheffield Council and is a dedicated historian of a city he first came to in 1974 as a 21-year-old student, and never left. It was he who first alerted me to the stories of the rat pits in a local pamphlet he discovered in Sheffield Library and the presence of slaughterhouses along the riverbanks. When we meet on a cold December day in the run-up to Christmas, he arrives with another rat story to tell.

From Castlegate, Lady's Bridge spans the river Don to a street called The Wicker which was historically where livestock was driven along to the market sites (and designed especially wide to accommodate the herds). In one of 42 arches underneath the imposing viaduct, Simon tells me, a huge riveted water tank was installed in the Victorian era to supply local factories from a nearby weir, replacing an open dam or millpond.

Once industry along the river started to shut down, the tank fell into disuse but remained in situ largely empty of water until the 1990s when Network Rail decided to remove it in order to lease out the arch. When they assessed the tank, however, they discovered rats had somehow burrowed inside and established a huge colony. So many rats were present, he tells me, that the pest-control firm Rentokil was invited to shoot a promotional film inside the water tank. For a time, the rats of The Wicker had the briefest of dalliances with fame.

Just as 200 years ago the people of Sheffield were seemingly relieved to see the stinking waters of the Sheaf buried beneath their feet, now, he says, is the time to open the site back up in a process known as daylighting and begin to restore the river's natural flow. Peering into a 1916-built culvert at the mouth of the Sheaf, Simon explains that the rushing sound we can hear is a large brick weir that prevents all fish passage upstream. Given there are now salmon in the river Don, the hope is that they can be tempted to recolonise the Sheaf, as long as enough man-made obstructions are removed. If the Atlantic salmon can make it all the way from Newfoundland to Sheffield, he tells me, the least we can do is ensure they are able to travel a few final miles upstream of the Sheaf to the city suburb of Totley, where there is suitable clean water and gravel beds to spawn.

We finish our tour standing on the eighth floor of a nearby car park, which offers an ideal view over the Castlegate site. Looking down at the strip of decaying concrete currently obscuring the river, Simon explains there will be far wider biodiversity benefits of deculverting the Sheaf, including improving invertebrate life and re-establishing the building blocks of freshwater ecology, which remains the most threatened habitat on earth.

Having been present on the site for 1,000 years or more, I wonder how the resident rats will adapt to this new vision for Castlegate? Over the course of that winter I make regular visits to the site as the bulldozers move in and begin to destroy their burrows on the old market. First, council contractors come along and strim back the buddleias where I have previously watched rats from the vantage point of a nearby alleyway. Within a matter of weeks the whole plot is levelled down to its concrete bones in anticipation of the landscaping work, with nowhere left for the rats to hide.

During this work, I begin to notice the bodies of rats littering the nearby cycle path that runs alongside the Don, presumably refugees from the Castlegate site seeking a new home. I remember what Shaunak Sen told me about the sympathy people afford rats in Delhi when their burrows are flooded during monsoon rain. No such amnesty is to be found here; the rats are running for their lives.

One day, while exploring possible rat routes nearby, I find a courtyard surrounded by a block of flats close to the river, in the centre of which is a planter flanked by communal bins. Probably 10 by 5 metres, the planter is pockmarked with fist-sized burrows. It is clearly an extensive network of rat tunnels. In 1962 John Calhoun compiled a list of tunnelling excavations from his own observations of captive rats in a pen. According to Calhoun, for a colony housing roughly five rats, there are on average 4.5 underground chambers, 16 tunnel segments and 6.8 exits. I count at least a dozen holes leading into the burrow. Based loosely on Calhoun's observations, that means at least 10 rats may be in residence.

While I am waiting in the courtyard, a resident comes out and lights up a cigarette and we start talking. She is called Maria and is visiting Sheffield from her native Greece, staying with her seven-month-pregnant daughter until the baby is born. She says the rats have recently become a lot more active in the courtyard. When she is outside smoking at night she watches them run across the ledges of the ground-floor windows and into the basement of the building. 'I don't mind them because it is just nature, I guess,' she tells me.

A few days later, I decide to come and see the rats for myself. I get there an hour or so before sunset and sit in the dark corner of a narrow set of stone steps leading to a blocked-up door overlooking the courtyard. It is a cold, wet evening and I huddle down in my coat and hood, peering at the burrows in the planter for signs of movement.

It is a part of the city populated by alcohol and drug users and as I sit quietly, several loud groups of drinkers walk past the gates outside on their way to a nearby off-licence. For a time a man on crutches with a blanket around his shoulders stands outside the gate smoking something with an unfamiliar and noxious chemical smell. As it grows dark, a movement-activated security light is set off every time someone walks past the courtyard, but nobody seems to notice me.

Despite it being early January, I watch several bats emerge from an unseen roost in the brickwork above my head. At this time of year they should be hibernating to preserve their energy but during warmer winters are increasingly rousing themselves to feed. I listen to the clicks of their echolocations and watch them swirl above my head, willing them back to bed for a long sleep until spring. Similarly, rat activity used to slow during the winter months but now in many cities it continues unbroken through the year due to rising temperatures.

A few hours after sunset I hear the first tell-tale rustle in the undergrowth and watch a dark shape emerge from the burrow and hug tightly to the edge of the planter as it travels in the direction of the nearby bins. It moves without hesitation, waddling forward with its nose pointing to the floor. Rats will often scent the markings of familiar routes to provide an olfactory map, and they possess a highly tuned sense of spatial awareness and muscle memory.

A short while later I spot another, darting from a large pile of cardboard recycling someone has dumped. Through the closed curtains of the flats inside I can see television screens flickering, their inhabitants cosily distracted as the rats come out to feed.

When you have been staring into the night for a while, your eyes start playing tricks on you. Some spiritualists believe that in the right conditions, doing so enables people to witness the dead. This is a process called a 'psychomanteum', whereby a person is instructed to sit in an enclosed, dimly lit chamber and stare into a mirror angled so they do not see their own reflection until eventually the spirits appear.

While the word itself is relatively recent (popularised in the 1990s by the US writer of the afterlife Raymond Moody), the process of eliciting shapes from the darkness is an ancient one. During his *katabasis* (a journey into the underworld in Greek mythology), Odysseus digs a deep pit into which he pours milk, honey, sweet wine and the blood of a sacrificial ram. As he peers inside, ghosts of his past swarm out to speak to him.

After three long hours perched upon the stone steps, I find I am no longer able to trust my own eyes. At one stage the security light clicks back on but as far as I can tell nobody has walked past. A fox, perhaps, or a particularly large rat? Under the lamplight I notice an odd shimmering within the undergrowth of the planter. Presumably it is just the light reflecting off fragments of broken glass, but for a moment it appears as if there are dozens of sets of gimlet eyes staring out from the rat burrows.

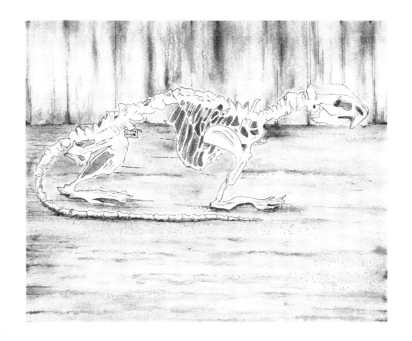

CHAPTER FOUR

Ratopolis

One of the striking things about rodent research is how relatively little we actually know about a species that is so ubiquitous. Far more effort has been expended attempting to expunge rats than trying to better understand their existence. As I am discovering, establishing exactly where and how urban rats live remains a source of some mystery. The biology and ecology of rats in a large city is a frustratingly under-researched subject. Mostly, we are happy to leave them to the shadows – until their secret world erupts into our own.

On 9 December 2017, a Parisian refuse collector opened a 600-litre blue industrial rubbish bin in an alley between

the Musée d'Orsay and the Pont Royal along the banks of
the river Seine. Inside teemed hundreds of rats, scrabbling
over one another and occasionally launching themselves
up against the moulded plastic sides of the bin in an
attempt to escape.

For the refuse collector, known only as David, his
discovery was the final straw. He uploaded the video as
evidence of the proliferation of rats along the Seine, telling
the camera that he and his colleagues now 'backed away'
from the bins each morning. The rats, he said, were 'truly
huge' and their presence a 'scourge' on the city.

It sparked something of a national debate about rats in
Paris, with politicians demanding municipal authorities
ramp up a city-wide process of what the French call
dératisation. As if such a thing could ever be achieved in a
place which, according to any number of deeply
unscientific studies (as nearly all such counts tend to be), is
one of the most rodent-infested cities on earth. After New
York, Paris is known as one of the great rat metropolises of
the western world.

At the beginning, at least, when Paris was founded by a
Celtic tribe in the third century BC, its connection with rats
was by dint of location. Situated at an important crossing
point of the Seine upon a marshy and agriculturally
productive river plain, the city's original Gallo-Roman
name, Lutetia, translates literally to 'swamp'. But over
subsequent centuries this reputation has taken on almost
mythical significance as the city's rodent population
boomed alongside its human population. As ever, where
skin and fur jostle together cheek by whisker, it is a
complicated relationship.

Parisian rats have been blamed for spreading plague and
pestilence and yet, during times of extreme privation, have

also become a delicacy in the famous capital of gastronomy. At the height of the Franco-Prussian war in late 1870, when allied German forces laid siege to Paris, cutting off food supplies, rats became a sought-after foodstuff.

The US physician Robert Lowry Sibbet, who found himself trapped in Paris during the siege and kept a diary documenting his experiences, describes roadside stalls displaying fresh rats on trays. Rat meat was priced higher than that of cat or dog. That Christmas, the now long-closed Parisian restaurant Voisin famously advertised one of the dishes on its festive menu: 'cat flanked by rats.' The same menu also had elephant and kangaroo on offer as the starving city pillaged its zoos.

At times Paris has declared all-out rat war, such as when populations that had boomed along the trench networks of the Western Front streamed back into the city alongside returning soldiers. In the summer of 1920, the now discontinued daily newspaper *Le Matin* described a 'grey invasion', with the city home to 3 million people and an estimated 8 million rats. In response, the city authorities pledged half a million francs (around £5 million today) to eradicate invaders described by one contemporary journalist 'as difficult to conquer as the Germans'.

But rats are also part of a far less adversarial side of the city. There have been moments in history when Parisians have viewed their resident rats with an air of protectiveness, almost pride. Occasionally, they have even seen their own lives reflected in the rodents' daily struggle for survival. In *A Tale of Two Cities*, Dickens describes the tyrannical aristocrat Monsieur the Marquis contemptuously viewing the working classes of Paris as nothing more than 'rats in their holes'. During the French Revolution, the long-maligned animal took on symbolic significance as a creature that, along with the city's working classes, had been brutalised by the Ancien Régime, but thrived nonetheless. This is encapsulated by the revolutionary folk hero Henri Masers de Latude, known for his swashbuckling tales of glorious failure: legendary prison escapes swiftly followed by inevitable recapture. During one prolonged stint in isolation in the notorious dungeons of the Bastille, Latude befriended the rats in his cell.

In his memoirs, he describes at first being tormented by the rats that nested in his straw prison mattress, biting him and running across his face at night. Realising he had no other recourse, he decided to befriend them instead. The Bastille rats immediately responded to his entreaties and soon became his closest companions. 'I owe to them the only agreeable relaxation I have experienced during the 35 years of my captivity,' he wrote.

Using scraps of bread and meat, Latude trained the rodents to perform tricks and submit to his strokes (although only around the neck, he stressed, never on the back as this would prompt the rats to lash out). Within a fortnight he had a 'little family' of 10 rats, which he claims responded to their individual names as he called out to them. His favourite was a female he grandly christened Rapino-Hirondelle (the second part is the French name for the acrobatic swallow).

His dungeon rats soon gave him more comfort than anything he had encountered in the cruelty of the human world above. 'I found myself in the midst of a family who loved and interested me,' he wrote. 'Why then should I wish to transport myself back into another hemisphere, where I had met with nothing but assassins and executioners?'

The release of the 2007 Pixar film *Ratatouille*, in which a Parisian rat with a taste for haute cuisine takes over the kitchens of a high-end restaurant, rekindled a modern love affair between the city and its rodents. When the film was first released in France it was reported there was a 40 per cent increase in people keeping rats as pets. However, humans are nothing but fickle in their tastes. Fast forward a decade or so and we are back at that swarming rubbish bin on the banks of the Seine, and a growing number of the city's inhabitants are calling for urgent action to rid Paris of its rats once and for all.

That same year the rodent-infested bin was filmed, in another part of the city a group of ecologists analysing small mammal activity in the garden connected to the Paris Museum of Natural History also started to discover rats appearing in the live traps they set. Previously during their research only shrews, wood mice and hedgehogs (of which Paris has an enviably sizeable population) had sprung the traps, but suddenly they found they were retrieving rats, and in considerable numbers. It was clear something was afoot: the rats were on the march.

This rodent invasion, alongside the growing animosity across Paris towards rats, prompted a collective of scientists to launch a new project intended to finally unpick the secret lives of the city's famous inhabitants. They cited three main objectives: to decode the biology and ecology of rats in Paris and use genetic testing to map the dynamics of populations, to better understand the diseases they carry and the risks of transmission to humans, and finally to help explain people's own prejudices towards rats. The name given to the project is fitting for an animal so regularly blamed for hastening humanity's demise: Project Armageddon.

It is a Sunday in March and I have travelled to Paris by train from London for an interview with some of the experts involved in the project at the Paris Museum of Natural History. I am staying with old family friends in a block of apartments near the Quai de Jemappes, but they are away on my first evening so I am left to my own devices.

To pass the time, I take a walk alone along the Canal Saint-Martin, which runs outside the apartment. Groups of young Parisian hipsters line the banks of the canal, built at the turn of the nineteenth century under Napoleon's orders, enjoying the last rays of the sun and final dregs of the weekend. Along the water's edge, empty bottles and food boxes pile up around the already overflowing bins.

I follow the canal until it leads to a small park where I quickly encounter my first Parisian rat burrows. They are humungous – the largest I have ever seen – and some the size of fox holes. Various black plastic boxes containing poison have been placed in the undergrowth, though resistance is evidently futile. The burrows form a sprawling network of tunnels, evidenced by a trench of heaped earth mined by rat claws running along the edge of the park.

I sit quietly, near to a group of men swaddled in winter coats swigging wine straight from the bottle and arguing loudly with one another. It does not take long for a rat to appear, and it does so with a suitably cinematic flourish. For at the very moment the avenue of wrought-iron lamp posts that line the park switch on for the evening to illuminate the city of lights, a rat sparks into life. I watch as it scuttles past the swings of a children's play park and darts underneath a pedestrian footbridge. It is a large, muscular specimen, and the speed and delicacy of its movement reminds me of the miniature Italian greyhounds I have just seen flouncing along the banks of the canal. Under the lamplight its long tail forms a calligraphic flourish as the rat races unseen past the squabbling drunks and a young couple half-heartedly playing pétanque with gloves on. Then it disappears into the cold night and the streets that until dawn are its to explore.

I realise the following morning that my trip has coincided with the all-too-fleeting moment every year that is always impossible to judge until you find yourself immersed in it: the beginning of spring. The morning air is crisp and cold and the sky so blue even the murky canal water shimmers invitingly in its reflection. The poplar and plane trees lining the city's avenues are beginning to burst into bud.

I arrive early at the museum and take a walk through the botanical gardens opposite. The poppies are in bloom, sparrows busy the trees and a few dozen people of all ages are taking part in an open-air tai chi session on the neatly combed gravel. Paris in spring, Hemingway once observed, when the city brims with unfulfilled promise. Although he neglected to mention the rats.

Inside the museum, Professor Christiane Denys meets me at the door of her office wearing a thick jumper due to the intermittent central heating. As she bustles about looking for mugs and apologising for her broken coffee machine, I notice on one of the desks a large specimen of a dead root rat. A palaeontologist by training, Christiane has studied rodents for decades. Originally from Lille, nowadays she lives outside the city and unless she is travelling in for work prefers to avoid the sort of dense metropolis where the subjects of her interest most thrive. 'Paris is not my cup of tea,' she tells with me a grin, after asking where I grew up. 'But London is a *terrible* city.'

Her research spans the breadth of the shared history between people and rats. Along with work conducted by other palaeontologists, Christiane has countered the well-spun narrative that rats are relatively recent invaders to the western world. In fact, she tells me, there is archaeological evidence of the black rat in Neolithic and Bronze Age communities, and she agrees that brown rats have resided in Europe for far longer than many people think.

As we talk about Project Armageddon, Christiane tells me her own theory about the widely reported Paris rat explosion of recent years. Contrary to popular perception, she suspects, the rat population has not changed all that dramatically. Rather it is human behaviour that has shifted, and the rats are simply reflecting that back.

The old Parisian culture of eating in restaurants at lunch is disappearing, she tells me, with a more transatlantic approach to fast food increasingly imported. People eat outside and drop food wrappers, which draws the rats out from their traditional spots. The aftermath of the Paris terror attacks of 2015 has also had an effect. To deter future bomb attacks the city authorities replaced bins with open containers where it was easy to peer inside (and for a rat to crawl). Christiane says she and colleagues are occasionally visited at the museum by refuse workers holding a squirming rubbish bag filled with rats, although these bins have in recent years started being replaced with larger, more secure containers designed to deter the rodents.

Increased flooding of the Seine is also believed to have encouraged sizeable swarms of rats, as their burrows become breached, forcing them to seek out new territories. Its marshy origins means Paris has long been susceptible to floods. During the Great Flood of Paris of 1910, parts of the city remained underwater for two months. That was the worst flooding to hit the capital for the past two and a half centuries and now these catastrophic events are becoming far more common. In 2016, three days of heavy rainfall deluged some of the city's main thoroughfares and prompted an emergency evacuation of artworks from the Louvre. Researchers from Oxford University and elsewhere have concluded that such natural disasters are now twice as likely as a result of humanity's influence on the climate.

We break off for a tour of the museum archives, which Christiane presides over in her role as curator. She leads me into a back room closed off to the public and filled floor to ceiling with stainless-steel filing cabinets. She pulls open the drawers to reveal neatly stacked bodies of Parisian rats dating back centuries. The rats are perfectly preserved, their fur still sleek and whiskers sharp and pointy. On closer inspection, though, their vital organs have been removed and eyes replaced with yellowing wads of cotton wool.

Each rat has a label tied to its foot detailing its own personal log of where it was collected and by whom. As Christiane explains the labels to me, a fantastically detailed zoological history emerges. She shows me one sizeable specimen (232mm long and weighing 255g), collected in a garage in the Cantal region of France on 2 April 1943. I find it oddly moving that in the midst of the Second World War and Nazi occupation of the country, somebody still found the time to collect an unusually large rat and send it in to the museum for analysis. As Europe starved, were they not tempted to eat it?

Other specimens date back centuries. Within the collection are rats gathered by Georges-Louis Leclerc, later known as the Comte de Buffon. A talented natural historian, in 1739 Buffon was appointed the first keeper of the Jardin des Plantes, the historic heart of the Museum of Natural History. The Jardin des Plantes also has its own interesting rodent history as the home of what is thought to be one of the world's first closed captive rat colonies (meaning one that is self-sustaining with its own offspring and does not have any outside animals added in). According to a recent academic paper on the origins of the brown rat, this colony of hooded brown rats (a breed of Norway rat) was recorded at the Jardin des Plantes from 1856 until 1988, and they were bred in order to feed the inhabitants of the reptile house in the gardens.

Among its archives, the museum also has collections by the eighteenth-century English naturalist John Berkenhout, the man credited with giving the binomial title *Rattus norvegicus* (or Norway rats) to brown rats in his 1769 opus, *Outlines of the Natural History of Great Britain*. Berkenhout describes the appearance of the rat plainly in the book: 'length to the tail 9 inches; tail 9 inches. Back tawny. Belly dirty white. Feet and legs almost bare. Tail scaly. Omitted by Linnaeus.' That last line is a veiled dig at fellow eighteenth-century naturalist Carl Linnaeus, a Swede known as the father of modern taxonomy.

Berkenhout was a famously meticulous man who worked as a doctor alongside his natural-history studies. However, when it came to his classification of the *Rattus norvegicus*, he made a mistake which has stood the test of time. The rat was named in the belief it had arrived in western Europe (or at least Britain) on timber ships from Norway. Instead, as we now know, the stowaway had arrived in Europe from Asia, and several centuries before Berkenhout and his contemporaries might have realised.

Alongside the bodies of the rats are neatly packaged collections of their skulls and ribcages. Christiane takes out one of the skulls to demonstrate to me how rats use their teeth. In the front are the four large incisors. Then there is a cavernous gap called the diastema where the rat fills its cheeks with food and discards anything it deems non-edible. At the very back, a set of 12 small molars works in a grinding motion to enable rats to chew their food into a pulp.

Those teeth are key to the evolutionary success of rats. A recent University of Liverpool study of rodent biting mechanisms found the ability of rats to both gnaw with their front teeth and chew with the back molars has given them the upper hand against other rodent species. While guinea pigs have evolved to chew and squirrels evolved to gnaw, the study found the rat can do both more effectively than the so-called 'specialist' species. This versatility is what makes the rat so destructive and has enabled it to so successfully conquer the world.

The muscles around a rat's jaw have also equipped it with a shockingly powerful bite. Rats exert roughly 150kg of biting force per square centimetre, which equates to around 2,000 p.s.i. For context, this is more powerful (relative to body weight) than a hyena, grizzly bear, bull shark or hippopotamus, and roughly 20 times the bite of a human.

These teeth represent both the rat's greatest strength and its Achilles heel. While their power and their ability to bite around 6 times per second means a rat can chew through nearly anything, they are also left with little choice. A rat's front incisors are open-rooted, meaning they never stop growing. Without continuously biting them down, these teeth will curl up like a ram's horn inside a rat's skull and ultimately cause it to die. Every rat, therefore, is born with a curse upon its head, to keep gnawing until the moment it perishes.

Holding the small skull in my hand it strikes me how often we fixate on the rat's incisors as symbols of its voracious appetite and savagery rather than the set of teeth at the back, upon which it actually relies to eat. This is part of the fascinating dualism of the rat: the outermost parts, which have evolved to enable it to survive in almost any conditions, predate upon animals and aggressively defend its territory, and a far more private and gentle inner world. Although that said, the elongated, curving rat skull does also remind me of Ridley Scott's *Alien*. Pity the rat, always having someone else's baggage projected upon it.

Christiane agrees. For her, one of the most important parts of the project is breaking down myths around rats and explaining to people how we might better coexist. She is dismissive of current attempts to limit or even wipe out rat populations with poison, pointing out that, worldwide, scientists have already discovered more than a dozen genetic mutations in rats demonstrating resistance to anticoagulants (the poisons most commonly applied in an attempt to kill them). She also stresses the high risk of secondary poisoning in other small mammals. 'Rats belong to an ecosystem and if you touch one part of an ecosystem you can destroy another,' she warns.

Crucial to breaking down these barriers, she says, is explaining to people that rats are not in themselves a threat to humans merely by their presence on the streets or in sewers. 'If this project can help find a good way of managing populations of rats, we can explain to people how we can live with them,' she says. 'The point is we need to explain how the rats live, what is their place and how we can manage them gently with ethical methods. If you know, you are less afraid.'

Back in her office we are joined by an ecologist called Benoît Pisanu, who occupies the distinguished role of chief rat-trapper for Project Armageddon. Benoît has worked with rodents for more than 30 years and studied exotic species (not to mention fleas, ticks and worms) across the world. Parisian-born, Benoît retains a particular interest in the small mammals residing in his home city, especially its rats.

What also attracted him to the project is the possibility of solving the great rat paradox that afflicts authorities not just in Paris, but across the world. Millions are spent in controlling populations without actually knowing what the rats are doing, and how and where they live and coexist.

And so Benoît and his colleagues went to trap rats. He tells me how it started the previous March. First they selected four green spaces in different areas of the city, chosen for their varied nature, ranging from relatively wild to intensively managed, and proximity to humans. They spent around three weeks trapping in each site, laying up to 100 live cage traps and setting them with a special bait Benoît has perfected over his years in the field: animal food pellets, peanut butter, sardine oil and sunflower seeds (irresistible to juvenile rats in particular).

They trapped the rats over spring and summer. Each captured specimen was weighed, sexed and checked for its reproductive status before being tagged and released back into the wild. This, explains Benoît, is to obtain precise information about the movement of the rats and to help compile statistical models calculating density and abundance. The final week of trapping was to sample rats for up to 20 diseases including Covid-19, leptospirosis and a host of hantaviruses.

Some rats were recaptured, but most quickly learned after the first attempt to steer clear of the cages. This is in stark contrast to other less intelligent rodent species, such as red squirrels, which, he says, will often stumble into the same trap twice within an hour.

Benoît typically works in remote locations and his presence in Parisian parks laying traps before sunset elicited a wide public response. He was also surprised by the number of rat defenders approaching him, checking that he was not planning to kill the animals he caught. 'People are either fascinated or frightened by rats but above all they are interested in how they live,' he tells me.

In between the live captures, camera traps were also used to monitor the selected locations. While stressing they are preliminary results, Benoît tells me the team were taken aback by their discoveries. Based on previous studies, they were expecting a minimum of 30 rats per hectare in the areas they monitored, rising to 100 rats per hectare in more extreme cases. Instead they found that even in the busiest locations, there were only between 6 and 12 rats per hectare. Roughly, Benoît says, the presence of rats was between 3 and 5 times less than they imagined.

They also found that, far from being widespread across the city, the distribution of rats is in fact very patchy and tightly associated with human activity. In the wilder green spaces they analysed, such as the Parc des Buttes-Chaumont in the north-east of the city, they only discovered rats present in one-fifth of the entire park over 20 days of trapping. However, this was also where they caught the largest rat detected in the study: a whopper weighing in at 471g (an average football, by comparison, is 450g).

The study shows a simple aspect of rat control that is continually overlooked in the rush to lay down fresh poison: where nature is left to itself and healthy ecosystems allowed to flourish, rodent numbers tend to automatically reduce or at least level out. Rather than rootling through bins for easy food in such locations, the rats discover they are very often the food source themselves, predated upon by everything from herons and foxes to owls silently swooping through the city night.

Benoît stresses that the data his team has gathered also tells us something important about perception. 'We always focus on what we see,' he says. 'When you see a rat, usually it is because they are already numerous, and so we only retain the moments when we see many. So everybody thinks there are many but it is not so true – there are many, many less than we think.' He breaks off and bangs the table we are sitting around for effect. 'It is very important to have this message. They are not that many and we can live with them!'

It was not always so on the land that today comprises the Parc des Buttes-Chaumont. When the 25-hectare park opened in 1867 it was hailed as the new green lungs of Paris, a place where the working classes could relax and stroll through nature. However, the park was also an attempt to redress the sins of the past, for the newly landscaped grass verges and flowerbeds covered what had turned into a suppurating ulcer of the city.

For centuries, this site housed the Montfaucon gibbet, the most notorious in France. The stone 10-metre-high structure was used by successive royal rulers and specifically designed to display the bodies, which were strung up in windows like horrifying department store mannequins, as a warning to the wider populace. The gibbet was finally demolished at the end of the eighteenth century, but arguably worse was to come. Montfaucon became the centre of Paris's sewage disposal industry, with truckloads of excrement carted up and dumped in old quarry pools on the site to be reused as fertiliser.

Montfaucon also housed a series of knackers' yards. Business was brisk and thousands of equine carcasses were rendered here every year. Workers toiled among bubbling vats of fat making tallow for candles and slipped across stone courtyards covered in blood and guts. Everything from meat to hair was salvaged from the corpses to turn into profit. When darkness fell, a nightmarish army of rats emerged to feed. In winter, when the corpses froze, the rats were known to burrow directly into the flesh and eat their way out from the inside.

Occasionally rat-catchers would be called, wading in with flaming torches and clubs and killing up to several thousand rats in a single night, but it made little difference.

Often the stench from Montfaucon would drift across Paris, and the site provoked a ghoulish fascination in chroniclers who visited to document this scene of horror. The French writer Théophile Gautier has a particularly vivid account in his 1838 essay, 'La Ville des Rats'. Where Naples had Vesuvius, he wrote, Paris has Montfaucon, from which every day a torrent of rats spews from its depths threatening to engulf the city. Worse still, he stresses, they are no ordinary rats. He describes them as of 'Herculean' proportions, 'as fat as elephants and as fierce as tigers'. Their teeth, he writes, are as hard as steel and their claws as tough as iron. Should any of these savage hybrids encounter a cat, he imagines, they could easily dispatch it in two bites.

Other visitors to the land surrounding Montfaucon described it as being so intricately woven with rat burrows that the ground echoed beneath their feet. Gautier pictures a subterranean 'Ratopolis', warning that when they have had their fill of horse meat, the rats could descend on Paris to feed on humans instead.

This was, as the English natural-history writer Edward Jesse (who also visited Montfaucon) described, a genuine fear of the city authorities. No matter the stink, the concern was that closing the slaughterhouses might inadvertently unleash an invading army upon Paris. A nineteenth-century lithograph stored in the archives of New York's Metropolitan Museum of Art depicts a horde of giant rats attacking three besuited men, who flap at the rodents with their umbrellas. The drawing is entitled the 'Great revolt of the rats de Montfaucon, which don't want their feed to be taken away by scientists'. But when the site was finally closed in 1849 and the park established in its place, there is little evidence of the city being invaded.

This hell was entirely constructed by human design. People built the gibbets and carted the exhausted horses of the republic on their final journey here. We lit the fires under the tallow tanks and boiled the carcasses into glue. Of course, rats moved in. Wherever humanity's impact is greatest upon the earth and the filth and detritus of our own creation is at its most destructive, you will find rats, too. They show us what we have done.

Wandering around the park today, past its landscaped bridges, lakes and immaculate flowerbeds, I find it impossible to imagine such horrors, not least as Benoît's trapping has revealed that most of the park is now largely absent of rats, thanks to people cleaning up the land and restoring it to nature. But then I think of the one 471g monster rat he caught somewhere here, and wonder whether he unwittingly discovered a relic of the past?

The architect behind the redesign of the Parc des Buttes-Chaumont was Baron Haussmann, a man who over the course of the latter half of the nineteenth century had been tasked by Napoleon III with tearing down much of the old

city and redesigning Paris along modern lines. As well as
eradicating the labyrinthian medieval streets and turning
them into the wide boulevards radiating from imposing
roundabouts which Paris is famous for today, Haussmann
was also focused on the very bowels of the city. He built a
modern sewer system which runs for more than 1,300 miles
under the streets. Or, as Haussmann described them in 1854,
'underground galleries' which serve as the 'organs of the
metropolis'.

These new sewers of Paris were of such interest to Victor
Hugo that he dedicates several chapters to them in *Les
Misérables*. 'Paris has beneath it another Paris,' he wrote. 'A
Paris of sewers; which has its streets, its crossroads, its squares,
its blind-alleys, its arteries, and its circulation, which is of
mire and minus the human form.' The ruler of this
'subterranean palace' he imagines to be the rat, a creature
Hugo argues is so ubiquitous in the city that it seems 'the
product to which Paris has given birth'.

The sewer, Hugo concluded, is the conscience of the city:
'Everything there converges and confronts everything else.' I
see rats in a similar vein. They are a creature that reveals to
people the overlooked truth of their own city; they are
emissaries from its darkest corners.

It is mid-afternoon when I leave the Museum of Natural
History, sunset only a few hours away. Benoît had told me
the most active period in their spring monitoring was the
hour before dusk. The rats of Paris will soon be stirring.

I walk along the Seine to the gothic sixteenth-century
Tour Saint-Jacques, which according to various media
reports has been overrun with rats in recent years. The

square surrounding the park is busy with homeless people crowding on benches and the bushes are strewn with poison trap boxes, but I see no rats. Evidently they have been driven out of what is a popular tourist spot. Later I notice a review of the tower on Tripadvisor written by a visitor from Tucson, Arizona, with the valedictory headline: 'The rats are gone.'

Around the corner from the tower lies Julien Aurouze and Co, said to be the oldest pest-control business in Paris, founded in 1872 and still going today. The shop's glass frontage displays assorted taxidermy rats that have been collected over the past hundred years or so in various states of misfortune. Some of the stuffed rats dangle by their necks from old metal traps, a modern-day version of the Montfaucon gibbet. The shop has become famous in recent years after briefly appearing in the film *Ratatouille*. Remy the animated rat is taken to the shop by his father, Django, who points out the poor critters swinging in the window and warns him what happens if rats get too close to humans. Their world, he cautions, is one that belongs to an enemy.

Once, though, the rodents of Paris had a tiny corner of the city to call their own. Indeed, you can still just about spot it carved into the limestone façade of the street corner of the Rue de l'Hôtel Colbert in the swanky fifth arrondissement. Now this narrow street opposite Notre-Dame cathedral on the left bank of the Seine is a place of discreet bars marked by box hedges and a chic hotel. Centuries ago it had a very different name: Rue des Rats.

At the end of the street on the river embankment is a row of the ubiquitous book stalls that are famously strung out along the Seine. I fall into a conversation with the seller facing out over the old Rue des Rats; he is sitting in a camping chair, reading a book and wearing a furry hat with ear flaps to ward off the cold. His name, he tells me, is Christian Nabert. Now 72, he has been occupying the same spot for 20 years. A lifetime spent reading outside is, he tells me, his idea of perfect happiness.

Over the years he has conducted his own research into the history of the Rue des Rats. The road is one of the few parts of old medieval Paris that survived Baron Haussmann's nineteenth-century modernisation and has appeared on maps of the city since at least the thirteenth century. The street, he tells me, was near to a butcher's row where carcasses of poor quality meat were hacked up and salted to sell to the city's poor. Rats inevitably followed and in such abundance that the street was named after them.

At some point in the nineteenth century, the increasingly well-to-do residents moving into the street (where apartments now sell for several million euros) decided the name was bringing down the area and protested to the city authorities that it should be changed to Rue de l'Hôtel Colbert. But history, as the French Queen consort Catherine de' Medici once noted, is written by the survivors. Blowing the steam off his Thermos of coffee, Christian tells me the story of Rue des Rats did not end there.

In 2019 the world was stunned by the images of Notre-Dame cathedral on fire. The thirteenth-century cathedral's spire, clock and oak-beamed roof were gutted in the blaze but in truth it was a miracle not more was destroyed. Ever since, the cathedral has been a hive of construction work as it is slowly rebuilt. The rat colonies that nested in the confines of the cathedral grounds have fled the commotion, Christian says, swimming to the opposite bank of the Seine where his stall is located. He points out to me the burrows they have dug in the tree pits along the street and at the very top of Rue des Rats. He, for one, is pleased to see them return. 'The rats are part of the city. It is a pretty dirty city and they belong here,' he says.

Construction is a key driver of rat movement in cities. Building works, laying roads and utility cables, demolition and construction can all uproot rats and send them scurrying off in pursuit of new homes. I have witnessed this sudden rat migration for myself, living in the town of Sowerby Bridge in the Calder Valley in my early twenties, where I started off as a trainee reporter on the *Halifax Evening Courier*. The council constructed a new swimming pool on the site of the old market, only a few streets from the house I rented. When the works started, there were widespread reports of the streets being swamped by rats streaming off the site to escape the demolition crews.

A few minutes' walk away from Rue des Rats is the Square René Viviani, a small public green space surrounded by busy roads, cafés and restaurants and exactly the sort of place Benoît has told me is most likely to be occupied by rats. It is around 5 p.m. now, the perfect spring day rapidly transforming into a cold March night and so I hurry to take my seat for the evening performance.

The park is presided over by an attendant and not long after I walk in looking for rat holes a shrill whistle pierces my ears. The attendant angrily gestures at me to step off the grass and so I choose a bench that offers a decent vantage point. Here I sit and watch park life pass me by. A man with a guitar on a strap around his neck is shouting angrily at a fountain in the centre of the square. Several homeless people cluster together on benches while others are occupied by couples talking quietly. La Sorbonne University is nearby and a few students mingle. Pigeons strut self-importantly past and a small flock of sparrows darts back and forth like children scattering across a playground.

Around 5.30 p.m. I see the first rat, and a big one too, loping through the undergrowth. Not for the first time watching a rat, I think what an almighty racket such a secretive creature can make, but no one else seems to notice.

It is clearly part of a colony that rules over this corner of the park. Over the next half hour or so I see six in total, sometimes exploring together and sometimes alone. A few of the rats are apparently juveniles that have just survived their first winter. As the minutes tick by the rats grow increasingly brave and at one stage I watch a squadron of four make a combined foray out through a patch of daffodils towards a bin. Less than a metre away three students sit on a bench oblivious to the creeping rats in their midst.

In my bag I have a box of macarons with which I am tempted to entice one of the rats, but I have noticed that the park attendant has been giving me increasingly quizzical looks so I restrain myself. At 6 p.m. sharp she blows the piercing whistle again and orders the last few dregs of us out of the park. Frozen cold with aching joints I go to the café opposite and drink a hot chocolate by its old ornate radiator with my cheeks flushed and fingers numb.

I think of Christian's words about the cultural importance of rats to Paris. Belonging is a curious term in a metropolis like Paris. I grew up in London and eventually left after concluding the city didn't mean as much to me as it once did. Or maybe it meant too much and I couldn't adjust to the constant change on the streets and memories of my childhood. Either way I often wonder what it means to belong in a big city. Houses and businesses are bought and sold, neighbourhoods demolished and rebuilt, and every day millions stampede through on their way to somewhere else. But that was the word Christian carefully emphasised to me: rats *belong* here.

In 1920, plague returned to north-east Paris with around 100 cases reported, mostly in some of the poorest parts of the city. The outbreak was part of the third plague pandemic, which originated in China in the nineteenth century and quickly swept the world. In Paris it became known as the 'ragpicker's plague' due to the concentration of cases among the unofficial street-litter pickers who lived in crowded urban slums and were largely Jewish refugees from eastern Europe or French colonial Africa.

Paris declared war on the rat, with the authorities organising a public bounty hunt offering the price of up to 30 centimes (about 3 pence in today's money) per body to rid the city once and for all. As citizens formed into vigilante groups patrolling the streets with dogs and clubs, an estimated 653,000 rats were killed. Some used guns, prompting local papers to run articles stressing the danger of being caught in the crossfire, while at least one hunter died after being asphyxiated by sewer gas. In eighteenth-century France the expression 'avoir des rats' (to have the rats) was used to indicate a person who had a 'touch of madness' about them. Suddenly, the whole city was in its grip.

Peter Soppelsa, a historian at the University of Oklahoma, has written an interesting article on the rat war. He cites the use of increasingly derogatory language towards rats and how quickly that turned into scapegoating of ethnic minorities. As he points out, the rats also had their defenders. Most prominent among them was the French socialist writer Fanny Clar, who in September 1920 wrote an article for the now defunct daily newspaper *Le Populaire* entitled 'Poor Rats!' Clar wrote of her pity both for the rats and the men and boys who had been cajoled into hunting them down. She questioned the social justice of sending the city's poorest into the least salubrious corners of Paris to kill rats, and the efficacy of the policy when, despite hundreds of thousands of rats being killed, plague cases were still on the rise. Eventually the city authorities agreed and over the course of the 1920s the rat war slowly receded.

A century on and the rat has once more become political in Paris. When I visit in 2022, the increased number of rodent sightings has emboldened opponents of the city's Green mayor Anne Hidalgo, who have seized upon the rat as a symbol of poor governance and decline. An image of a rat has also been mocked up above the five Olympic rings as a symbol of how the city's sanitation problems might threaten the games when they host them in 2024. With many on the centre-right calling for a new rat war in Paris, the rhetoric has become so aggressive that during one council meeting Douchka Markovic, a Parisian councillor and co-president of the animal rights political grouping Parti Animaliste, suggested rats should be renamed *surmolots* instead (a biological name for the species), saying the term 'rat' encourages violence.

Markovic was laughed at in the chamber and widely mocked on social media afterwards. Following her appeals for rat clemency, the French National Academy of Medicine released a statement emphasising that rats do pose health risks and should be treated as such. But history shows Markovic has a point. The very language associated with rats does indeed engender violence, often bringing out the worst in us.

Pest control in Paris is dictated by the central mayor's office, although each district in the city also has its own individual mayor who operates with more limited powers. In 2018, one such mayor, Geoffroy Boulard, who presides over the well-heeled seventeenth arrondissement and is a centre-right opponent of Hidalgo, decided to take matters into his own hands: launching an interactive map showing the extent of rat infestations in his district and helping form a 'citizens de-ratting brigade'.

I meet with the mayor one morning in Paris at his office. Downstairs is organised chaos as his staff rapidly muster donations to Ukraine following the Russian invasion a few weeks previously, but upstairs I am ushered into a plush room with leather seats surrounding a glass table. I am kept waiting for 45 minutes until the besuited mayor bustles in, apologising profusely for the delay. He spreads out a copy of his rat map on the table before explaining to me his battle plan.

Geoffroy, who is in his early forties and works as a business consultant alongside his mayoral role, tells me he was moved to act after an infestation of rats prompted the temporary closure of two nurseries and a school in his district. He started visiting other cities to see what control measures were in place, including New York, where he met the chief of pest-control management and Eric Adams, the then mayor of Brooklyn and later mayor of the whole city.

Adams has a well-professed hatred of rats and in late 2022 posted an advert for a city 'rat tsar' to help reduce its rodent population. The job posting called for someone who is 'highly motivated and somewhat bloodthirsty' with a 'swashbuckling attitude, crafty humor and a general aura of badassery'. I wonder if he noticed these were personality traits that could equally be applied to the rats themselves? Either way the new director of rodent mitigation was being offered up to $170,000 a year to lead the city's new zero tolerance approach.

While Geoffroy was in New York, he was shown an extermination technique he has now imported back to the streets of Paris: killing rats by placing small frozen cubes of carbon dioxide in their burrows. As the ice cubes melt the gas evaporates and slowly asphyxiates the rats as they sleep. 'I have done it myself,' he insists. 'It is not cruel and very importantly it is safe for all the other animals.'

Like the Museum of Natural History ecologists, he is concerned at the risks of secondary poisoning and stresses that, unlike his municipal predecessors of the 1920s, he is not motivated by blind hatred of rats. 'We need rats underground,' he says. 'They have a function for the regulation of our waste. I'm not against rats because I hate them. I love animals and nature, no problem. The problem is the problem of public health.'

The first year Geoffroy launched his map, 2018, he received more than 3,000 reports of rat sightings. Over the three subsequent years that number has dropped by more than 70 per cent. Part of that, he says, is the work of the rats committee he established, which meets once a month with representatives of the district's parks, landlords and schools in attendance. And also there is the work of the citizens' brigade, a volunteer group of around 20 local residents who have mobilised with the intention of killing rats.

They call themselves La Brigade de Rats le Bol (a play on words, as *ras le bol* means to have had enough) and its members range from estate agents to stay-at-home mums, retirees, a comedian and a professor. I am put in touch with one of the brigade's most active members, a businessman called Jacques d'Allemagne. He tells me they don't have a uniform but sometimes wear red hats to identify themselves to members of the public and always wear gloves to handle the dry ice safely.

We never have a chance to meet in person but what follows is a long WhatsApp conversation that spans more than a year. Among the many articles and opinion pieces Jacques sends me about rats are photographs and videos of infestations the brigade has investigated. One is filmed by someone walking into what appears to be the laundry room of a block of flats. A few rats leap up disturbed from their burrow and are followed by the camera as they scale a pipe like trapeze artists. It demonstrates the physical ability of the creatures. I never ask what happens to those particular rats, but I can guess.

On my last day in Paris I find myself again walking through the city, mapping out some of the historic changes in the street patterns that had been explained to me during my trip. Stopping occasionally to check the modern-day routes against an old copy of a map displaying pre-Haussmann Paris, I find myself drawing lines in my mind between the modern and ancient city that do not correlate to either map. This is the rat's life of flux. Left to their own devices they will follow the same paths over generations. You can see these well-trodden routes sometimes in patches of flattened grass leading to rat burrows, or sunken lanes ploughed through urban scrub that rats use on their daily commutes. But these ratlines are only ever traced upon a city, as they are compelled to adapt to a constantly changing urban landscape.

I stroll through Le Marais, whose narrow, winding streets were left largely untouched by Haussmann and show how the city once was. *Le Marais* means 'the marsh' in French. Now these once fetid streets teem with tourists. From there, I head along the Place de la République, a centrepiece of Haussmann's project and, like many of the new city streets, deliberately constructed to be wide enough so garrisons of soldiers could be quickly mustered to quell any municipal unrest. In between these tangles of the old and new, I also spot recently established campsites in local parks, many of which I presume to be refugees either evicted from the camps at Calais or on their way over to the coast. I walk to the constant pounding of pile-drivers hammering into seemingly every street corner in a constant, ceaseless cycle of progress. New buildings are thrown up, others razed to the ground and all the while the city scurries past.

I have one final appointment before I leave Paris and it is back at the Museum of Natural History with Professor Bertrand Bed'Hom, a specialist in evolution and genomics. He is involved with what I find to be the most interesting and novel part of Project Armageddon: studying the rat population of Paris using genetic markers. Basically, Bertrand explains, questioning whether the rats are the same the city over. It may sound simple but it is something nobody has ever fully investigated.

So far their work, he tells me, has revealed something rather surprising. Instead of all rats genetically overlapping, as one might expect given their spread across the city and prodigious breeding, they appear to be genetically distinct, depending on which neighbourhood they reside in. They are preliminary figures, Bertrand stresses, but if ultimately confirmed it could drastically change the way we think of urban rats.

This would mean that rather than constantly mixing and inter-breeding as is generally assumed, in fact colonies of urban rats are tethered to their neighbourhoods (and have been for centuries). As Bertrand says: 'It looks like there is not one large population of rats in Paris, but several small families in one territory.' Generally the rats of Paris live in the neighbourhoods where they were raised and defend them fiercely against incomers.

Such is the pressure on rats – not least by attempts to control them – that there will be extinction-level events for individual colonies, which will see rivals move onto their turf, but often, Bertrand says, this will mean moving only a few hundred metres. He contrasts this to the return of the wolf across France, which has been reintroduced as part of rewilding efforts, and is a long-distance migrant that can cross miles of new territory in a single day. 'Probably rats are very local animals,' he says. 'If you see evolution of human populations, it is the same.'

I leave this meeting with my perception of rats utterly shifted. Walking back through the busy streets I grapple with this idea that rats, too, have their own neighbourhoods which for generations they have fought over and defended to the hilt. If anyone or anything belongs in a city, it is them.

It also explains the limitations of widespread municipal responses to panic at rats being sighted in any particular urban area, and also the folly of attempting to eradicate a colony in a particular part of the city without addressing the environmental factors that enticed them there in the first place, as a new family of rats would simply move in and become entrenched.

In June 2023, the Paris deputy mayor for public health announced that a committee was being established to consider the prospect of 'cohabitation' with the city's rats. This marked a significant departure from previous policies of *dératisation*. While bitterly opposed by opponents of the mayor Anne Hidalgo, the decision could herald a new dawn in Paris's relationship with its rats.

Wilder parks and gardens, improved sanitation and housing in the poorest parts of cities, greater biodiversity and above all a nuanced understanding of how rats live is becoming increasingly clear to me as the answer to how we deal with them in modern conurbations. These old families of rats have dealt with humans coming at them with sticks and flaming torches, the city being levelled and rebuilt around them, and have endured a campaign of prolonged hatred that has spanned the centuries. It all passes on, this terrifying experience of human interaction, flows through the genes like the maps of the shadow realms they have long inhabited. But rats need us, and whether or not the feeling is mutual, we are stuck with them.

CHAPTER FIVE

Heroes and Villains

Cohabitation was also now part of my daily routine. Back home we were gradually growing accustomed to one another, the rats and us. They were increasingly happy to leave their cage and explore around various rooms of our house. Their favourite spot was an upstairs study where their feet would pitter-patter over the bare floorboards as we tapped away on our computers, and if we were not careful they would nibble house plants and pilfer pieces of paper to shred.

We had taught them to bob for frozen peas floating in a ramekin of water, a game in which they appeared to take particular delight. We could also get them to rise up on their haunches for food. In between completing these tasks, both were becoming very affectionate and would scuttle up to us for tickles.

Both Liz and I were aware early on of a sense of the rats watching us and adapting to our lives. They would listen out for when we were going to bed, knowing that feeding and play time was imminent. As we walked up the stairs to their cage they would excitedly fling themselves against the bars as a puppy bolts to the front door. They would also wait until we had woken up in the morning before going to bed themselves. Any change to the routine – if we were having building work in the house, or guests – and they would demonstrate their displeasure by toppling their food bowl over onto the bottom of the cage.

As they matured, the rats were becoming far more mellow around one another and their play fights less frequent. They groomed each other, slept huddled up close and spent a considerable amount of the day (and night) chewing cardboard to line their nest, in between attempting to locate each other's secret caches of food around the cage.

Despite being the more dominant of the two, Ermintrude was inherently more cautious and also less agile. Unlike Molly, who could effortlessly scale the top of their cage and along our arms, Ermintrude would struggle slightly to haul herself to the top. The exception to this was whenever we vacuumed near their cage and she would immediately scamper towards the noise.

At first, I thought this might be Ermintrude emphasising her role as the boss rat and putting up a spirited defence against a perceived threat. But she never seemed stressed or aggressive when she did so. You may well question how I could even know this but detecting a rat's mood is less opaque than some might imagine. Studies have demonstrated that their facial expression changes with their emotions. In analysing the adverse response of rats to unpleasant laboratory experiments, scientists have dubbed this the 'rat grimace scale'. It works the other way, too. When rats are enjoying themselves their eyes shine bright, ears turn a porcine pink and droop and relax.

Ermintrude would move quite steadily in response to the vacuum, in a manner unlike her normal ratty leaps. As she hopped between the levels of the cage, rising up and down on her haunches, she also bobbed her head. After a few months of watching this behaviour, I encountered an intriguing theory. It was based on a study by researchers at the University of Tokyo, who had examined the influence of rhythm on rat movement. In the study, the researchers fitted 10 rats (and 20 human volunteers) with wireless devices that measured their head movements, then played one-minute excerpts of Lady Gaga, Queen and Mozart's *Sonata for Two Pianos in D major* at different speeds. The hypothesis was that rats would prefer quicker music due to their organs working at a faster rate to humans, but in fact the researchers discovered both species most enjoyed music of exactly the same tempo – 132 beats per minute, otherwise known as an allegro – and would dance along in time.

The rats in the study displayed an innate enjoyment of music and instinctively moved in time to its beat. Previously this was a trait scientists presumed was unique to the human race. Maybe, I wondered as I read it, the motorised hum of our vacuum cleaner was prompting Ermintrude to dance?

Yet our training still remained in its infancy, especially so given the overall capabilities of rats. On the internet I had been watching videos of performing rats that put our own efforts to shame. One woman in the US had taught her rat to play basketball and paint pictures, which she displayed on miniature easels. At the University of Richmond in Virginia, scientists have taught rats to drive tiny cars. For the past half century at Nebraska Wesleyan University there has even

been a Rat Olympics (now rebranded the Xtreme Rat
Challenge over copyright warnings), where rodents compete
for gold medals in long jump, hurdles and rope climbing.
One day, I discovered the most impressive training
programme of all: a project harnessing rat intelligence to
save human lives.

During the Second World War, a new medal was struck to
honour the heroism of animals serving on the frontline.
Instigated by Maria Dickin, the social reformer and founder
of the charity the People's Dispensary for Sick Animals
(PDSA), the medal was intended to acknowledge
'outstanding acts of bravery or devotion' displayed by any
creature serving with the armed forces or civil defence units
in any global theatre of war.

The PDSA Dickin medal was first awarded on 2
December 1943, honouring three pigeons who had each
individually assisted in the rescue of RAF airmen (during
the war it was commonplace for homing pigeons to be
deployed alongside crews, with an estimated 250,000 birds
in service). One of the pigeons, Winkie, had been aboard a
Bristol Beaufighter when it crashed into the North Sea
following a raid over Norway. Unable to radio to mark their
position, the crew instead released Winkie from the sinking
aircraft in a desperate attempt to seek help.

The pigeon managed to fly 120 miles back home over the
roiling sea to reach Broughty Ferry on the river Tay where
her owner raised the alarm with the nearby airbase, RAF
Leuchars. A search-and-rescue team was scrambled to their
position, pinpointed by measuring the time difference from
the plane ditching to the arrival of the pigeon, as well as the

wind direction and air speed of the bird. Incredibly, due to Winkie's endeavours, the bomber crew was rescued. Later they held a special dinner, with Winkie attending in a cage as guest of honour. In the autumn of 2023, a bronze statue of Winkie was unveiled in Broughty Ferry.

Over the ensuing years the PDSA Dickin Medal, a bronze medallion inscribed with 'for gallantry' and 'we all serve', has been awarded to a host of animals in conflicts including Bosnia, Iraq and Afghanistan. This roll of honour comprises roughly 40 dogs, 32 pigeons, 1 horse and a solitary ship's cat, who have all been presented with the prestigious medal known as the animal Victoria Cross. And then, in 2020, they gave it to a rat.

Strictly speaking, the rat in question, Magawa, an African giant pouched rat, was given the PDSA gold medal (the non-military equivalent of the Dickin medal), although he earned it risking life and limb in the most deadly of conflict zones. The medal was awarded for Magawa's 'life-saving devotion to duty, in the location and clearance of deadly landmines in Cambodia'. At the time of his award, Magawa had sniffed out 39 landmines and a further 28 pieces of unexploded ordnance in a country still dealing with the ruinous legacy of successive conflicts. During the Vietnam War, the US dropped millions of bombs upon Cambodia. Following the ousting of Cambodia's genocidal Khmer Rouge regime by invading Vietnamese troops in 1979, a further 4 to 6 million landmines were laid across the country. These munitions still litter the countryside today, claiming victims among the civilian population. Cambodia is home to an estimated 40,000 mine amputees (the highest ratio per capita anywhere in the world).

Magawa was the leading light of a team of mine-detecting rats deployed to the country in 2015 by the Tanzania-based charity Apopo. To date, the rats have helped release more than 33 million square metres of land in Cambodia to make it safe for public access. Magawa alone personally cleared 141,000 square metres. Not for the first time, rats are cleaning up humanity's mess.

Time, however, nips at the heels of even the most heroic of rats. In January 2022, Apopo announced the death of Magawa after he had reached the venerable age of eight. He had already retired the previous June after beginning to slow down and lose the speed which in his prime would enable him to search a football field's worth of mines in 20 minutes (a task that would take a person with a metal detector an estimated four days to complete). Over the course of his career, Magawa had retrieved an estimated 100 landmines.

His demise prompted a flurry of headlines across the world and an outpouring of grief among his sizeable social media following. The announcement also came only a fortnight before I was due to fly out to visit the Apopo headquarters in the eastern Tanzanian city of Morogoro. The timing of my arrival was purely by chance. I had arranged the trip long before news of Magawa's death, hoping to meet the next generation of mine-detecting rodents, and had been waiting for international travel to resume following the latest bout of Covid-19 lockdowns.

The plane was practically empty, with only a couple of masked passengers dotted across swathes of seats. The journey was a night flight and even with several rows to myself I struggled to sleep. Instead, to pass the time I watched an action film called *Suicide Squad*, on the advice of a friend who told me that rats played a starring role.

They are led by a woman called Rat-catcher 2, a sort of pied piper figure who uses a beacon of light to control rats. She was taught her skills by her heroin-addict father, who raised her on the streets of Porto. In one flashback he sits with his daughter on a rooftop overlooking the Portuguese city, stroking a rat and insisting that, despite their maligned status awarded by humans, they have purpose too.

The story of a supernatural person able to amass hordes of rats runs deep through our culture. A nineteenth-century illustration entitled 'Spying on a sorcerer with her rats' depicts a small blond boy hiding behind a tree staring at an enchantress sitting by an open fire with a column of albino rats marching towards her. The seventh-century Flemish nun St Gertrude of Nivelles is considered the patron saint of rats and was often depicted with rodents crawling upon her. The same theme connects these stories over the centuries: what if we could somehow summon rats to do our bidding?

The story of Apopo and its rats started in 1995 when the charity's Belgian founder, Bart Weetjens, started investigating possible solutions to the scourge of global landmines and discovered an article about gerbils being taught to sniff out explosives. Even considering the discerning nose of any rodent, rats possess a particularly highly-tuned olfactory sense. It has been discovered that they have around 2,070 smell receptor genes, which is a third more than mice. Weetjens had bred rats as a teenager, occasionally hiding treats for them around his house, which they quickly retrieved. He contacted a friend from university in Antwerp called Christophe Cox with the outlandish theory of training rats to become bomb-detection squads.

After consulting experts they were told that of the more than 60 species of the genus *Rattus*, African giant pouched rats would be the most suitable for the task. Native throughout much of sub-Saharan Africa, the rats grow up to around 3 feet (1 metre) snout to tail. They weigh on average around 1kg and yet, despite their hefty size, are still light enough to step on a landmine and not set it off. They are long-lived, the eight years Magawa reached is typical for the species, and possess a calm temperament, making them easy to train and habituate to humans. Also, like all rats, they will do almost anything for food; even run over a minefield.

Bart and Christophe established some rat kennels in an old industrial unit in Antwerp and, after partnering up with the rodent specialists at Sokoine University in Tanzania, were sent their first batch of giant pouched rats. It did not go as planned. The imported rats arrived unruly and wild. They fought among themselves – sometimes to the death – and proved difficult to train.

The second batch arrived more settled and in 1998 Bart and Christophe managed to breed their first litter of giant pouched rats in captivity. They trained the litter of three pups using a method previously established with hooded brown rats to successfully seek out a canister of explosives in laboratory experiments.

At the turn of the millennium, Apopo moved to Sokoine University. Here, on the green and sprawling campus in the shadow of the Uluguru mountains, the charity has developed the most extensive training minefield in Africa. Magawa's legacy looms large over Sokoine University. In one entrance hall a wooden plinth bears a photograph of him wearing a tiny rat-sized replica of the coveted PDSA medal, with a certificate honouring his life-saving work.

I am greeted at the main drive by Lily Shallom, the communications manager for the charity, who is standing next to a flat-bed truck embossed with the slogan: 'We train rats to save lives.' As the person in charge of Apopo's social media outputs, Lily was at the centre of the maelstrom following the announcement of Magawa's death. Their

Instagram account @herorats has more than 60,000 followers, who delight in the regular updates of the Apopo rats. Some even pay monthly instalments to 'adopt' one of the rats.

Magawa, Lily says, was an 'excellent rat and just made for the job' but he already has something of a successor in another, unrelated rat, Ronin, who has recently been deployed to Cambodia. In total the programme has around 40 breeding rats and a constant line of succession ensuring the mine-detectors of the future.

Lily grew up in Morogoro with a Dutch father and Tanzanian mother. She studied at university in Holland and speaks perfect English with a hint of an accent that could be either Dutch or American. She is a passionate birdwatcher but equally enthused by the rats. After six years of working together, their affections and intelligence continue to surprise her.

Training commences, Lily explains, once rat pups are around four weeks old and beginning to fully open their eyes. Once cognisant, they are immediately habituated to human contact. She introduces me to one worker, Albert, whose job it is to play with the rats every day. We watch as he tickles a litter of four seven-week-old rats in a plastic box filled with sawdust shavings. Their fur is not yet fully grown and I can see the outline of their sinewy muscles as the youngsters clamber onto the edges of the box. Albert scoops them out in turn, stroking them and letting them run up his arm.

The rats are entirely unperturbed by human contact, and that is the point. Despite their impressive size, like all rodent species giant pouched rats are naturally skittish, especially so with noise, and there are various tasks they must complete in order to ensure they are ready for the minefield. One of the more extreme training exercises is to be placed on the hood of a car while the driver honks the horn and fires up the engine. Only when a rat can endure this task (one, it is worth stating, that is approved by animal-welfare officers) without so much as flinching can it progress to the next stage of training.

Similarly, it is vital that Apopo staff are fully relaxed around rats. In job interviews, candidates often have a rat suddenly dumped upon their shoulder to see how they respond. Lily says the previous day she posted a video of Albert playing with the rats on social media. 'It went completely nuts,' she grins. Many people posting in reply wrote about how rat tickling would be their dream job. For others, I imagine as I watch the young rats writhe over one another and squirm their way out of his grip, it would be a nightmare.

The next stage of training features explosives. Lily leads me to some soil-filled boxes roughly one metre square where larger juvenile rats are put through their paces. We watch as one male rat in a green harness is released into the box. Buried somewhere in the depths is a tea egg, a metal infuser in which loose tea leaves are placed, although this particular device is filled instead with TNT.

The rat trawls across the surface of the earth, its whiskers twitching and snout close to the ground. Every few seconds it stops to wash itself; the ever scrupulous rodents don't like dust coating their whiskers. Within moments the rat has located the tea egg and begins digging with its paws down towards it. As soon as the egg has been located, a trainer sounds a clicker and the rat scampers over for its treat, a syringe filled with an avocado and banana smoothie from which it greedily sucks. Then the tea egg is reburied, the earth flattened with a trowel and the process begins again. The rodents slowly progress through ever-larger training soil boxes before they are deemed ready for the 24-hectare field within the university campus, containing 1,500 (deactivated) landmines and other explosives hidden within it.

Training on the field begins early, before the heat of the day has taken hold. The rats are collected from the kennels, weighed, then placed in wooden boxes lined with sawdust and bussed down a dirt-track to the minefield. Here their feet and ears are slathered in factor 50 sunscreen before their harnesses are attached to leads. In the wild, the giant pouched rats are nocturnal and live mainly in underground burrows, so are ill-adapted to prolonged sunshine. Even this early in the day the rats can only spend a limited amount of time outside.

Fanning out across the minefield, the Apopo rats adhere to the same process of scurrying and scratching. The charity operates a strict policy of positive reinforcement in their training methods. The rats know from an early age that a successful discovery of a mine will lead to more food. In total it takes around nine months to fully train a mine-detecting rat and it is estimated they can work in the field for up to five years. As well as Cambodia, Apopo's rats have also been deployed to Angola, Mozambique and Zimbabwe.

The kennels where they live are a rat's paradise. There are rows of large cages, and play cages where the rats mix together (although male and females are separated to ensure no unwanted breeding occurs). They sleep in clay huts that mimic their burrows in the wild and there are ropes to climb and wooden scratching posts on which to keep their teeth and claws in check.

Alongside their reward of avocado smoothies, the rats are fed a mixture of fruit, vegetables, powdered milk, oats and imported rodent pellets, crushed into a paste. As an extra treat they occasionally receive the sun-dried sardines known as dagaa that are popular throughout East Africa.

Every Friday after training the centre hosts a weekly event called 'full-cheek Friday' at which the rats are treated to a special feast and squeak with delight as the food is served. The name is taken from the gluttonous nature of the rats, who can stuff considerable amounts of food into their cheek pouches to save for later while still eating.

Despite the several hundred rats living here, there is no smell in the open-air cages, and Lily explains that their droppings are changed every couple of days and turned into the most fabulous compost for the centre's fruit and vegetable garden. Back home I had never used the droppings from our pet rats for compost, imagining them as reservoirs of debilitating disease, but after discussions with Lily and several rodent specialists at Sokoine University I was assured that these raisin-sized poos were in fact perfect compostable material – not least as they come with paper, card and wood, which the rats have already pre-shredded. I have sworn by the method ever since, spreading the decomposed rat muck across my garden and allotment. As I am rapidly learning at Apopo, where we overcome our prejudices it provides space for our relationship with rats to become far more mutualistic.

Lily then takes me to the kennels for retired rats where the rodents that have already served with distinction in the field are allowed to live out their days in peace. Six is the average retirement age although some, such as Magawa, serve longer. A few grizzled rats, grey around their mouths and with patchy fur, slink into their huts when we arrive. Lily says as they get older they become more solitary. The previous Christmas she had tried to involve some of the retired rats in a promotional photo shoot but they barricaded themselves inside their huts with rocks, insisting on being left in peace. At night the rats will still chatter to one another between their cages and sometimes, if they are deemed lonely, will be moved to share another cage. Mostly, though, the elderly rats prefer a contemplative existence.

When they die, Lily says, they are buried on site but not in a marked grave, to avoid offending the staff working at the centre. The rats are also buried on a weekend when there are fewer people around. In Tanzania, Lily explains, burials are expensive with communities asked to chip in, and it would not be right to do for an animal what some cannot afford for family or friends. More broadly across East Africa, people tend not to share the western view of domesticated animals as cuddly extended members of the family. Keeping cats and dogs as pets, for example, especially in more traditional rural areas, is a rarity. Cats in particular are often associated with witchcraft and kept well away from the home.

The prevailing belief among staff working at the centre, Lily explains, is that the rats do not have souls and therefore it would be culturally offensive to afford them proper burials. As someone raised in Tanzania but educated in Europe before returning home, and therefore exposed to these two very different cultural appreciations of animals, I wonder what she thinks about the possibility of a rodent soul? 'I don't think they have them in the same way we do,' Lily replies. 'But they are definitely beautiful creatures.'

The highly tuned senses of rats has led to them being regarded as oracles. The sixteenth-century philosopher

Francis Bacon once observed that 'it is the wisdome of rats, that will be sure to leave a house somewhat before it fall'. Rats can alert us to sinking ships and tunnels on the verge of collapse. Back in 373 BC, the Ancient Greek historian Thucydides noted rats (as well as dogs, snakes and weasels) deserting the city of Helice several days before it was destroyed by a catastrophic earthquake. Rats can also smell human disease, detecting the subtleties of the inner workings of our own bodies long before symptoms appear.

Alongside their mine-detection work, the Apopo rats are also utilised in a well-developed tuberculosis-detection programme. TB is one of the leading causes of death from infectious disease in Africa, and the number-one killer of HIV-positive patients due to their already compromised immune systems. The continent has roughly 25 per cent of global cases and yet detection rates remain low.

The main technique used to detect TB in clinics across Tanzania (and indeed across much of Africa) is something called smear microscopy, which involves a clinician analysing the sputum of patients. It is a process that takes roughly two hours and has a detection rate somewhere between 20 and 60 per cent, meaning a high proportion of TB-positive patients are misdiagnosed as healthy and continue to spread the disease without seeking treatment. A far more accurate method, endorsed by the World Health Organisation, is a machine called a GeneXpert, which works at a molecular level. However, the high cost of the cartridges required by the machine and the fact that it needs to be kept cooled by air-conditioning can make it prohibitive in an environment where power is intermittent and funding scarce.

Rats provide a cheap and accurate alternative. The Apopo rats can sniff out the compounds produced by the bacteria that cause tuberculosis on samples at a speed and precision far greater than human detection. One rat can check around 100 samples in 20 minutes. Overall the rats have a detection rate around 40 per cent higher than clinics.

Despite early proof of this concept, Lily admits it has been a struggle to persuade the medical community. Medical-detection dogs are an increasingly well-accepted diagnostic tool for a range of diseases including cancer, Covid-19 and Alzheimer's, and yet the idea of incorporating rats is, for many medical professionals, beyond the pale. 'There is a lot of scepticism the animal can be more effective than humans,' Lily says. 'They also have a reputation for being dirty, which they are not … I guess the rats just have a bad rap.'

Slowly, however, the accuracy and consistency of their results have persuaded some of the detractors. While initially it was a struggle to get a single local clinic to sign up to the TB programme, now Apopo has partnered up with 80 clinics across Tanzania. Since 2007, the rats have screened more than half a million samples.

Every day a fresh batch of samples arrives in Morogoro, transported by motorcycle courier in ice boxes from the Tanzanian capital Dar es Salaam, a five-hour drive away. Before the TB samples are submitted for testing, they are heated to 100°C in a pressure cooker to ensure the rats cannot be accidentally infected. Then they are placed in slides in a glass-fronted metal box into which a rat is released.

I watch a rat called Campbell (all the Apopo rats are given names) being put through his paces by a few technicians. When he correctly identifies each TB sample, which he does by holding his snout over it for three seconds, as they are taught in training, he is presented with a syringe of food through a hole, which he greedily licks before getting back to work. In 12 minutes he checks 70 slides, confirming every one that has already been identified by the laboratory who sent the TB samples over, and finding 13 extra. A human technician, by contrast, would typically manage eight samples in a day.

Apopo estimates its rats have prevented in excess of 120,000 potential TB infections that otherwise would have slipped through the net. And yet, despite the longevity of their findings, the scale of the project and the huge gains in speed, cost and accuracy of detection, they still struggle to gain the acceptance of rats as a viable alternative. The World Health Organization has refused to endorse their work, which for now remains classified as 'operational research'.

Another Apopo project, which is closer to being incorporated in an official capacity, is a relatively new sideline in which the rats are used to help counter the illegal wildlife trafficking trade. From East Africa's port cities (and in particular Dar es Salaam), illegal shipments of everything from rhino horn to elephant ivory to tiger carcasses and pangolin scales are transported principally to Asian markets, where they are used for traditional medicine, food, fashion or ostentatious displays of wealth.

Rats are already in their first phase of training and have progressed from sniffing out pangolin to elephant tusk and rhino horn. The week I visit, a meeting is scheduled with the port authorities in Dar es Salaam to see how the rats might be deployed in the shipping containers being loaded onto cargo vessels. While port officers are susceptible to bribes to let shipments pass through, the rats are unimpeachable. In time they could prove to be an unstoppable force against wildlife traffickers – a creature blamed for so much environmental destruction helping reverse the fortunes of some of the most endangered animals on earth.

There is a final Apopo project I am invited to catch a brief glimpse of before we leave. Near the minefield, a building has been set up to resemble the rubble of the aftermath of an earthquake; filled with planks of wood and heaps of broken furniture and electronic detritus. As I arrive, a Scottish behavioural scientist called Dr Donna Kean and a team of researchers are following a rat with a backpack snaking between the chaos.

It is one of seven Apopo rats being trained as a search-and-rescue specialist to be deployed in the aftermath of natural disasters. While dogs tend to skirt the perimeter of ruined buildings, the idea is that rats can squeeze in through the smallest of spaces to search for survivors. The rats wear a backpack containing a camera, a two-way radio to its trainers outside and a precision geo-locating device. When they reach their intended human target they pull at a switch around their necks to alert their trainers and then trot back out to safety for their reward of food.

The researchers are still concerned about how a human, even in their most desperate moment, might react to being rescued by a rat. To counter any negative reaction, researchers are considering adding a recorded message to the rat's backpack that plays when a person is discovered. The message, I'm told, would be something along the lines of: 'I am a trained rescue rat and I'm here to help you.'

Watching the different Apopo training programmes, I am struck by how if we overcame our aversion to rats they might be incorporated into our lives, to our benefit as well as their own. I picture an alternative world where rats on leads could join soldiers on night patrols, helping warn them of explosives in their path, and deployed in ever

greater numbers to sniff out the landmines that maim
civilians across the world. Not least now in Ukraine where
swathes of new minefields have been laid across the Russian
defensive lines. I imagine arriving at an airport and seeing
sniffer rats on leads inspecting people's luggage, and hospitals
having a diagnostic rat wing freeing up overstretched health
staff to adopt more public-facing roles. As global disasters
become ever more regular as a result of climate change,
teams of search-and-rescue rats could help free humans
from the ruins.

The intelligence, adaptability and willingness to work to
our benefit (as long as there is a continual supply of food)
are all there. The main hurdle to overcome is human
prejudice. If we can achieve that, they may soon need to
start striking many more rat-sized medals.

I have come to Tanzania to witness both the best and
worst of rats. For outside of the Apopo training facilities
in the densely populated urban and rural communities
across Tanzania, rodents are also a daily blight on people's
lives. Housing conditions in the poorest parts of Morogoro
and beyond create the ideal situations for rats to thrive.
People live alongside rubbish tips and open sewers; whole
families sleep packed into a single room with earthen
floors and tin roofs, which rats can easily access. They steal
food, bite children in their sleep, attack poultry and spread
disease.

Elsewhere on the Sokoine University campus, away from
the Apopo kennels, a group of scientists are plotting their
demise. The Institute of Pest Management is the most
developed rodent research facility in all of Africa, whose

staff are devoted to investigating the extent to which rodent-borne disease is spreading through the population and devising new methods to keep rats at bay.

The institute is headed up by Professor Rhodes Makundi, whom I meet for an interview in his office one morning. Born in Kilimanjaro and now in his late sixties, Rhodes undertook a PhD at Newcastle University in the early 1980s, and speaks in a soft, almost whispered voice. Regarded as one of the leading specialists in the world, he is a well of rat stories: from the time he used a chainsaw to slice a rat-infested mattress in half to preserve the elaborate tunnels they had woven through the stuffing, to the endemic rodent species in Tanzania forced to move habitats ever further up mountains as a result of climate change. Their diminishing habitats Rhodes describes to me as becoming 'island ecosystems in the sky'.

There are more than 120 rodent species in Tanzania. Many cause little or no problem to the human population. Species like the African soft-furred rat (a mountain dweller Rhodes and a research team discovered in 2013) exist in remote locations, munching predominantly grasses and seeds. But there are three species considered serious menaces in terms of decimating crops and spreading disease: the African giant pouched rats; another endemic African species which is called a mastomys and is more of a large field mouse, and the black rat (*Rattus rattus*), a foreign invader thought to have first arrived in East Africa on the sailing ships known as dhows belonging to the Arab traders who plundered these lands many centuries ago.

Unlike northern Europe, in the warmer climes of the Mediterranean and sub-Saharan Africa the black rat still thrives. Smaller and more nimble than brown rats, they are particularly adept at climbing and can waltz elegantly over the most vertiginous routes.

A few years ago, staying in a cottage on holiday in Corfu, every night we witnessed a family of black rats pirouette through the trees above us and perform a trapeze act along a washing line leading to a laundry room. Also known as roof rats, black rats will exploit any holes in a building to gain access. Their proximity to people means they are also extremely effective reservoirs of zoonotic disease (where pathogens can leap from animals into humans).

According to the World Health Organization, rats (both brown and black) are responsible for causing more than 400 million infections in people each year spread through bites, the fleas they transport, urine and their breath. In West Africa, rats are the vector for lassa fever, an ebola-like acute viral illness that infects up to 300,000 people each year, causing around 5,000 deaths. Their fleas are also responsible for regular outbreaks of bubonic plague in several countries across the world.

In Tanzania, Rhodes and his fellow researchers are particularly focused on leptospirosis, a bacteria that spreads through rat urine and is estimated to cause around 1 million cases and 60,000 deaths a year. The most lethal strains can have a mortality rate of around 40 per cent while the disease can leave people crippled. Rhodes says their research has confirmed the presence of the bacteria that causes leptospirosis in about 30 per cent of black rats tested. They have also detected other novel viruses similar to lassa fever, although none so far that has mutated to spread to humans.

The interaction between humans and rodents is not, of course, a new problem, but it is getting worse. As we talk over coffee, Rhodes shows me old colonial papers from

1912 which describe 'a plague' of rodents heading from east to west across Tanzania, decimating crops as they went. In recent decades, Tanzania's booming population (which has at least trebled since the 1960s to more than 61 million people) has gobbled up ever more wilderness to convert to agriculture. That is a story repeated the world over. As we lose more wild spaces and the animals that thrive in them to artificially irrigated monocultural farmland, it creates the ideal conditions for generalist species like rats to expand alongside us. 'We are becoming closer and closer to the rodents,' Rhodes tells me. 'It is not the rodents coming closer to us.'

Rhodes's team is helping coordinate a project – the first of its kind in the world – alongside Professor Steve Belmain, a US-born rodent specialist based at the Natural Resources Institute at Greenwich University. In something of a modern-day pied piper story, they hope to drive the rats not just from people's homes but out of their villages altogether through a community-wide systematic cull.

The researchers have identified two clusters of 12 rural villages in Tanzania and Madagascar to take part. In each country, six of those villages are being provided with 5,000 rat traps in an attempt to purge them of rodents, while the other six are being left as a control. Those communities taking part will be encouraged to continue rat trapping in perpetuity. As rat populations diminish, the researchers will test for rates of leptospirosis and other pathogens. If successfully proven to drive down rates of disease, the hope is that the project can transform methods of rat control in the developing world.

Simple as it sounds, the project is not without risk. Any mass die-off of rats could force their fleas to seek out new human hosts. In Madagascar, the 12 villages involved in the project are in the country's plague zone (albeit a less-affected part). Professor Steve Belmain tells me they will be taking precautions such as setting up flea traps (basins of water with floating candles) to monitor any prevalence of disease.

The project area in Tanzania is a series of interlinked remote villages on the border of the Udzungwa Mountains National Park and surrounded by sugarcane plantations. It is a six-hour drive from Morogoro into central Tanzania and I sit in the back of Rhodes's jeep.

As we rattle over potholed roads I stare out the window at the sights of rural Africa. Roadside hawkers sell barbecue meat at busy junctions, labourers swish at the fields with scythes and traffic police in spotless white gloves wave us past an upturned truck whose cargo is rapidly being unloaded in order to clear the road. Rhodes has an old MP3 player plugged into the stereo uploaded with his favourite Motown and country music, so I watch all this to a backdrop of Kenny Rogers and B. B. King.

Eventually we turn off the paved road onto a dirt track running to the villages in the project area. On one side of the road loom the Udzungwa Mountains and on the other the villages stretch out alongside an endless sprawl of sugarcane plantation where the forest has been hacked away. Dotted in between the villages are dormitory blocks for workers bussed in to help secure the mammoth harvest. With their natural predators, such as snakes and birds of prey, driven deep into the remaining forest, the rats will have flooded the sugarcane fields, Steve assures me. Sure enough, as we check in to our hotel that night, I spot a furtive black rat scuttling across the restaurant floor.

In the morning we drive down a half-built road constructed on the orders of the former president John Magufuli (an avowed Covid denier during the pandemic who ended up succumbing to the virus) to visit the villages involved in the project. This whole area has been carefully chosen by the research team because of its unique geographical position. The mountain range parallel to the road provides a natural barrier to the west, while to the east a trainline runs to the copper mines on the Zambia border. In between, the rats are trapped in a sugarcane alley. For the researchers it makes them easy quarry.

At the first village, Mkula, we attend a meeting with the elders and are then invited to disperse the hundreds of traps we have brought over from Morogoro. We walk over a football pitch surrounded by banana and teak plantations and patrolled by squawking chickens, while children recite lessons in Swahili from the nearby school. The houses are largely constructed from mud bricks with open windows and corrugated tin roofs. As we start chatting to people, it transpires the villagers are suffering from an epidemic of rats. Some bear the scars of their nightly encounters.

The first person I meet, a young woman called Asha, who lives with her two children aged 6 and 13, tells me every night half a dozen or so rats crawl into her house through holes in the walls. They ransack the kitchen, crawl over their beds and mosquito nets, spraying them with urine, and occasionally bite.

Outside Asha's house, sitting under a tree wearing his Sunday best of red trousers, polished loafers and a white shirt, is farmer Pascal, who is similarly plagued by rats. Pascal is a single father with four children aged between 5 and 21. His children are from three different partners, none of whom he has been able to marry. The first, he explains in a quiet, lovelorn way, was banned by their respective families because she is a Muslim and he a devout Christian. The second left him. Because of his meagre earnings from working in the fields, he couldn't afford the dowry required by the family of the third.

And so he lives with his children alone in a mud-brick three-room house. He invites me in to point out a large rat burrow in the floor in the middle of his kitchen. He also holds up his 15-year-old's blue school uniform, recently ripped to shreds by rats. Pascal shows me an angry red welt on his finger where he was bitten by a rat the previous week. He caught three of them eating a bar of soap in his house and when he tried to shoo them away, one lashed out. He says he has been bitten three times in the past year alone, and shows me a vivid scar on his leg where he was attacked in his sleep. 'I was scared so the first thing I did was crush the rat with the back of my hand,' he says.

Pascal talks me through his day. He wakes up at 6 a.m. and walks to the fields known as the 'shamba' about 3km from his house. He works there until noon, when he returns home and prepares lunch for his children. He returns to the fields until nightfall and then treads wearily home once more to cook dinner. They eat ugali (maize flour), vegetables and occasionally, if he can afford it, some dagaa fish.

Out of his salary, there is no money left for rat prevention. On a good day a farmer can make about 3,000 Tanzania shillings (roughly £1) working in the fields, while a small packet of zinc phosphide rat poison costs about 1,000 shillings. Pascal has spent 2,000 Tanzania shillings (about 75p) on a local woven basket trap but even if he catches 10 rats it makes little difference. Ultimately, he says, he feels 'helpless'.

Walking around the village, I find everyone has a similar story. Children, I discover, are particularly susceptible to rat bites as they often go to bed with food on their hands and faces, which attracts the rodents. Normally the rats lick it off, but if disturbed they will bite.

In another nearby village I meet rice farmer William and his three-year-old son, Stuart, who three months ago was bitten by a rat that climbed inside his mosquito net. Ever since, Stuart has bolted in terror on the regular occasion he sees a rat. William's other teenage sons have so far escaped being bitten but his wife, Zwena, has been diagnosed with typhus (a rodent-borne disease which, if left untreated, can have a mortality rate of 60 per cent). Others in the family have been wracked with mystery fevers suspected to be associated with the rats.

In Mkula, even the local witch doctor has a rat problem. Kanoti, an amazingly youthful 78-year-old dressed in a white shirt and cloth cap, shows me the soles of his sandals, recently chewed by rats. 'That makes me very angry,' he scowls.

We sit outside the hut where he lives, a pile of seeds that have been hollowed out by rats on the floor between us, as the witch doctor tells me his theory about the plague that has befallen the village. He tells me conspiratorially that not all the rats are migrants from the sugarcane fields. He insists some have been summoned by witchcraft into the village by residents seeking to plague someone who has wronged them.

Kanoti also claims some power of control over the rats. Sometimes he is approached by a customer asking him to dispatch some into the home of an enemy. Occasionally people come to him to seek treatment from rat bites. He shows me bundles of mystery twigs and leaves in his hut that he uses. He also applies honey direct from a beehive to fresh rat bites, which he says can heal them. 'With rat bites I need to see if the rat was sent to you with a good or bad motive,' he says. 'If it is a bad motive then I must call the spirits to help me lift the curse.'

We distribute two main types of trap around the villages. The first are modern spring-loaded snap traps intended to kill instantly, which the project has ordered in bulk. There are also a few older, hinged, box-style traps known as Sherman traps, which are taken from the university stores. The traps were designed in the 1920s by Dr H. B. Sherman (who served in the US Marine Corps during the First World War, which no doubt gave him ample opportunity to develop his prototype). Steve and Rhodes insist that unless everybody is trapping rats the project will not work so we hand out hundreds, along with blobs of peanut butter bait, before promising to return the next morning.

That night, as traps are sprung around the villages, I sit drinking a beer with Steve. Originally from Maine but long settled in the UK, he is good company and opinionated on a range of subjects, but most animated when discussing rats. Over his years as a rodent expert he too has endured his fair share of bites, though he tells me he still remains in awe of his subject and delights in near-constant rat chat: from their extraordinary physiology to skewering urban myths. The largest rat he has ever performed a field autopsy on weighed 700g and the contents of its stomach alone weighed 200g.

He dismisses the old adage you are always within 6 feet of a rat, and is also highly dubious about the idea of a 'rat king' tied together by its tails. However, he insists stories of rats clambering up sewage pipes while people are sitting on the toilet are true. Steve also claims that even in the modern day, rats remain remarkably successful stowaways, existing on one-third of all maritime shipping.

Despite a career largely devoted to attempting to eradicate them, he is a lover of rats. 'I'm fascinated by them,' he tells me. 'The complexity of problems with rodents means you have to be a biologist, ecologist, anthropologist and bring all these things together.'

As a veteran on the frontline who has worked across the world killing rats, he admits that humanity will in all likelihood never win its war. However, he insists that we should still redouble our efforts. 'If we spent the same amount of money on rodent control as malaria control it would have a hundred times the impact on people's lives,' he tells me. 'Rodent control has much more potential to transform people's lives than pretty much any other development programme we have.'

I am braced the following morning to return to a scene of devastation. When we arrive at Mkula the rats have already been gathered up from people's homes and are heaped outside the village hall in a grisly grey pile. In order to catch live rats from which to take surgical samples, the older Sherman traps have also been used. The rats caught in there that are not required for testing are shaken out into a cloth bag and bludgeoned to death in front of us.

The black rats are surprisingly light, with white bellies and pale brown fur. Steve tells me that in medieval Europe they changed their colour to adapt to the mud and murky conditions, but here they need to be brown to blend in. Such is the rapid reproduction of rats that evolution and adaptation comes fast. And death, too, by the looks of the sickening scenes unfolding around me.

The researchers and villagers, however, appear altogether unfazed. Total eradication, after all, is a key tenet of the project and when an animal has caused as much misery as the rats do here, I suppose it is natural to afford them little mercy. In their shoes I would probably feel the same.

Some of the dead rats are dissected on field tables to retrieve samples to return to the laboratory in Morogoro to be tested for disease. I watch one autopsy of a rat that has been dispatched by being placed in a container of Halothane (a powerful gas used in anaesthetics) and pinned by its paws to a rubber mat.

Normally I tend not to be particularly squeamish. It is a prerequisite of being interested in any animal, and especially urban scavengers. But when the rat's stomach is sliced open I feel a wave of nausea rising up in me. I knew the basic anatomy of rat and human was broadly similar (hence rats are used so prominently in medical research) but hadn't grasped until that moment just how closely related we truly are. Lying prostrate on its back, the rat organs, ribcage and intestines are all so close to our own. I marvel for a second at its anatomy, immediately so recognisable and familiar, and the similarity between us and them. And then I am forced to look away for fear of being violently sick and walk off to the shade of a nearby banana tree until the medical examination is over.

Ridding villages of rats is no quick job. We stay on the sugarcane strip for several days, travelling up and down the road distributing the traps and returning the following morning to gather the bodies. At times the heavens open with intense tropical showers and the local river surges into a torrent, flooding the road. By the end of our stay we have witnessed the death of hundreds of rats. Those numbers will ultimately go down as populations reduce, but the project is running for several years and villagers have been instructed to maintain the intensity of trapping to prevent the rats returning.

While it is harrowing to see so many wild animals killed, hearing the stories of the damage the rats are doing to people's lives is equally shocking. I leave hoping they will manage to keep their villages rat-free in perpetuity, and thinking of the absurdity of our overblown western reaction to rats when we occasionally see them in a garden or park, rather than clambering over us in the night as is happening here. Centuries ago, before the advent of modern housing in rich developed countries, this presumably would have been our own experience with rats as well. Perhaps that explains the cultural aversion that has persisted to the present day. The scars of rat bites evidently take many generations to heal.

On the long drive back to Morogoro, as the countryside flashes past and Rhodes plays Linda Ronstadt in the front, I turn over in my mind the rats I have encountered in Tanzania, both saviours and destroyers of worlds. This is the same dichotomy as the human condition. Our earliest religious frameworks and moral codes revolve around the idea of light and dark. The question of whether our nature is somehow inherently good or evil underpins the earliest stories we tell ourselves. I think of the sweet, benign nature of the Apopo rats and indeed my own pets at home, compared with the near-demonic savagery of those in the stories I've heard in the villages we visited.

And yet this moralistic fixation on nature squeezes out the influence of context. And that is what I take away from the rat-fields of the Udzungwa Mountains. Those sprawling sugarcane plantations are an artificial environment created by us. Like swathes of countryside across the globe, they have been hacked out of virgin forest to maximise efficiency of food production to bolster an ever-growing population and sell for profit abroad. Wild animals have been expunged, habitats eroded and competing plants strangled with herbicide. The creation of such a sprawling environment entirely subverted to the benefit of humanity is all rats will ever require to thrive, for their needs are our own.

And so with each tree felled, drainage channel excavated and barrow of agricultural fertiliser tipped upon the earth, their numbers swell with ours. The victims are the people caught in the middle. Required to toil every day in the fields to maximise productivity and feed their families, yet unable to profit enough from the global food system they underpin to secure better accommodation and more sanitary living conditions that would keep the rats at bay. I think back to what Rhodes had told me earlier in the week – through our destruction of the environment we are coming closer to the rats, not the other way around.

Back in Morogoro we have one final neighbourhood to visit where rat-trapping is taking place. We head to Chamwino suburb, a sprawling shanty town and one of the poorest in the city, which is particularly prone to rat infestation. Here there is no running water, open sewers course through narrow alleyways and houses are built out of anything people can find: tarpaulin, straw roofs, bricks and scaffolding poles utilised as roofing joists. A few years ago there was a cholera outbreak in the city and the epicentre was in Chamwino.

A crowd has formed in advance of our arrival. It is early morning but a man on a bike holding a large hessian sack already appears to be extremely drunk and shouting at anyone who crosses his path. He stares at us aggressively through narrowed, bloodshot eyes as we walk over.

Traps were distributed across the neighbourhood the previous day and the animals caught in people's homes have been carefully laid out under the shade of a tarpaulin for us to inspect: 14 black rats, 3 mice, 1 shrew and an African giant pouched rat that is still alive and shivering in the corner of a cage it was lured into using hunks of jackfruit as bait.

The person in charge is Hussein Ramadhani, a mechanic and father of five who appears to be something of a community leader in Chamwino. He waves away the angry drunk and dozens of children running around us and invites us to his house.

We sit outside around a small wooden table where two teenagers are fixing together pieces of mobile phone and other electronic devices to resell by the roadside. In cages across the alleyway are chickens, with a fresh clutch of chicks running about in the dust. Hussein says the rats will attack them in broad daylight and kill them by biting their necks. He illustrates this by grimacing and drawing his finger across his own throat.

He also points out to me a shared toilet in a shack next to the house, which is a truck tyre planted into the ground as a seat with a latrine underneath. The African giant pouched rat they have just caught has apparently been undermining the toilet by burrowing underneath. Do the rats bite people, I ask? He laughs: 'Oh, they bite.'

It rapidly becomes apparent that the Sokoine University researchers have something of a negotiation on their hands. Hussein and his neighbours insist that they plan to cook the captured pouched rat for supper that evening. The researchers, on the other hand, are keen to save this one for the Apopo breeding programme. Discussions continue for some time in Swahili. Eventually it is agreed that the scientists can take the pouched rat away with us. While I do not see it, I presume some money changes hands.

We leave with the rodent in a cage ready for a new life in the Apopo kennels. Wild rats cannot be retrospectively trained as mine detectors because they have already developed too strong an aversion to humans, but they can sire offspring that are incorporated into the programme. In time, I hope, this hapless creature, rescued at the eleventh hour from the pot, might just go on to help save a human life in return. It is a fate that reveals the narrowest of margins between heroes and villains.

CHAPTER SIX

Quarry

All life washes up at Camden Market's Hampstead Lock. Tourists perusing the food stalls sit here to eat and take photographs. Starlings dash like pickpockets between the old willow trees overhanging the water, their poo streaking the cobbles and the occasional unfortunate passer-by.

Bloated binbags, polystyrene blocks, Costa Coffee cups and broken pieces of wood all converge in an evil-looking green slick at the base of the canal lock gates. On the opposite side of the water a fashionable couple in their twenties kiss and take selfies as a dead fox bobs in the lower sluice gates below them. The air smells of cigarette smoke, cinnamon from a nearby Dutch pancake stall and bacon fat. Irresistible, I imagine, to the no doubt sizeable local population of rats.

I have been waiting for 10 minutes or so when a ghost emerges from the throng. He is dressed in brown boots, brown trousers and an unbranded brown anorak with deep pockets. Beneath a green flat cap he sports a bushy beard streaked with grey. By his side scurry two small terriers, one brindle coloured with a white belly and paws, and another all white aside from a black spot above her left eye. I say 'ghost', but it is more as if he has simply appeared from another age. He is Matthew Blackwell, official falconer of Camden Market, and one of the last of London's traditional rat-catchers.

We set off along the Regent's Canal in the direction of King's Cross. The dogs, Monty (a Patterdale cross border terrier) and Gracie (a parson Russell terrier), tear in front of us through the tourists ambling by. When the dogs stray too far, Matthew calls them back with a long, low whistle. 'They're in there,' he tells me as Monty identifies a rat burrow in a flower planter and begins digging down into the earth. Few of the tourists eating lunch on benches around us even seem to notice.

Today, however, is not a rat hunt. Matthew has already spent the morning scaring off pigeons around Camden Market with one of his two Harris's hawks. One of the birds is named Gary (in what I assume to be a first for the species) and the other, Spencer. After resting up the hawks, Matthew has come to meet me at the canal to exercise the dogs and demonstrate their skill in tracking down their quarry. The burrow identified, he calls off the search and we carry on.

The dogs track countless unseen foes along the canal. After frantically digging towards a suspected rat burrow beneath a canal-side electrical junction box, Gracie attempts to launch herself through a fence towards what Matthew presumes is a foxhole before he quickly calls her back. They are different to any of the other dogs trotting up and down the towpath; not aggressive so much as wild. Like Matthew, they spend their working lives in corners of the city where few others dare to tread. 'That is the thing I enjoy most about my work,' he tells me as we walk under an old canal bridge where nesting pigeon squabs cheep amid the supporting steel girders. 'It is the places it takes you.'

Aged in his early thirties, Matthew speaks with a broad Kent accent, peppered with swearwords. He still lives in his home county with his partner and three children, and travels all over London in pursuit of rats. The son of a rat-catcher, Matthew always wanted to carry on the family business. Even after attending boarding school, where he says he was awarded a place because of his profound dyslexia, he had little interest in pursuing what he describes as a more 'illustrious' career.

A keen student of the history of rat-catching, he relishes the stories of some of his more famous Victorian predecessors and proudly continues their work. He is also fiercely critical of modern-day pest-control techniques, which rely upon poison rather than using it as a last resort. Traditional rat-catching, he insists, is a trade as worthy as any other, and one that requires a degree of skill many don't appreciate. 'If it was that easy to catch a rat,' he tells me he often thinks in the presence of some of his more disparaging clients, 'you would have fucking done it already'.

After first starting out working with his father, seven years ago Matthew set up business on his own and acquired and started training the dogs. Their formative experience in learning to kill prey, he says, was dealing with a mouse infestation at a branch of Poundland. From there they progressed to rats and are now lethally efficient. When rats are attacked they will leap up and bite the faces of dogs, so terriers quickly learn to strike hard and fast, shaking the stricken rodent in their jaws until it succumbs.

A few months ago, while working to curtail a major infestation of a rooftop bar in south London, Matthew tells me, they helped catch 60 rats over the course of two nights. A few days before we meet, he has been dealing with an infestation in a private school in London where they caught 15 rats.

Despite being involved in what is a largely solitary occupation, Matthew is an excellent raconteur. I pose the same questions I suspect he has been asked many times before, but he is generous with his time and happy to chat away. No, he has never been bitten by a rat. Yes, he believes rats are getting bigger (he puts this down to a fatty diet foraging in the sewer). The biggest rodent he has captured, he estimates, was roughly the length of a forearm.

The worst encounter Matthew ever had with a rat came when he was called out to a restaurant near the Natural History Museum. As he was exploring a roof cavity, a large rat fell through a panel and landed with a thump on his chest. The manager shrieked and slammed the door, leaving Matthew and the rat alone in the room. Eventually, he managed to stamp it to death.

Most rat stories, I have discovered, finish abruptly. But despite the inevitably brutal endings of their encounters, he insists a rat-catcher should always have respect for their quarry. He tells me he is in awe of the way rats adapt to human environments in order to survive, of their cooperation within colonies and savagery towards rival groups. He points me towards one fascinating study conducted by US researchers in the early 1990s, in a controlled experiment of laboratory rats in burrows, which demonstrated how rats raise the alarm to alert their own colonies. When a cat was introduced into the open area of the burrow system, the rats retreated into their tunnels and screamed ultrasonic alarm cries at 18–24 kHz, beyond the hearing of most adults but presumably deafening to a rodent's ear, for up to 30 minutes. When a lone rat not associated with any colony encountered a cat, however, there was no such cry. As he tells me this I wonder about the rat screams echoing out along the burrows of the Regent's Canal in Gracie and Monty's wake.

After dropping off the dogs at Matthew's car, where a shop owner on Camden's busy high street lets him park for free out of his admiration for the Harris's hawks, we head for a cup of tea. His unusual work makes Matthew something of a local celebrity around the market and the café owner greets him warmly and gives us a discount.

Sipping our teas, we talk more about poison. Matthew will occasionally resort to bait laced with poison but only after he has already employed the dogs, used traps and attempted to secure any access holes where rats are getting in. He has previously worked for other pest-control firms and is appalled at the indiscriminate use not only of poison but also of glue traps, sticky boards designed to trap rodents alive.

The traps are being banned for public use in the summer of 2024 but are still permitted to licensed pest-controllers in certain conditions. Matthew has seen the effects of the glue boards – where rats will sometimes gnaw off their own limbs in desperation to escape – and thinks they should be banned outright. He is also highly critical of the use of aluminium phosphide. The poison, which is permitted for licensed use across the countryside, is distributed in small pellets that release a lethal gas when reacting with moisture on the ground. 'What are we doing still using that?' he asks as he sips his mug of lady grey. 'Are we in the dark ages? It's a ridiculous chemical ... I've seen it used before and there is no life after that.'

Working once on a major infestation at a recycling facility in Greenwich, Matthew encountered a rare black rat. It was the only time he has ever seen one and, despite culling several hundred brown rats in the same facility, was careful to leave what is one of the country's most threatened small mammals alone. 'I felt quite privileged to see something so rare,' he says. He may kill animals for a living, but he recounts the experience with the excitement of any naturalist.

The mid to late nineteenth century marked the era of greatest celebrity for Britain's rat-catchers. In 1835, a new Animals Act was introduced that banned some of the most popular blood sports of the time, including bear-baiting, dog-fighting and cock-fighting. But 'ratting' was permitted to continue and quickly filled a vacuum. To meet the demand from a public that still wished to see animals tearing one another to shreds, pub landlords across the country erected rat pits in their parlours, basements and back rooms. Here people could bring their dogs to fight against a pack of rats while those present bet on how many the dogs could kill.

The rat pits were dens of iniquity that became hugely popular among all classes of society. And business boomed for rat-catchers, who were suddenly called upon to supply hundreds of rodents each week. The likes of Jack Black, who described himself as official rat-catcher to Queen Victoria, and James Shaw, a boxer turned pub landlord who ran one of London's most popular rat pits, became household names on the streets of the capital.

Their dogs also developed celebrity status in their own right, appearing on posters and being stuffed by taxidermists and displayed in glass cabinets once they had died. One such poster I've come across was printed at the end of the nineteenth century to celebrate the life of a terrier named Jerry, belonging to a Leicestershire pub landlord called Tom Withers and described as the 'Champion Rat Killer of all of England'. The poster details Jerry's greatest 'performances' in the rat pits, which included winning the All England Sweepstake in the Christmas of 1891, where he killed 14 rats in one minute and seven seconds at a pit belonging to a Mr T. Palmer in Birmingham. Jerry went on ratting for another six years before his final performance, taking part in a silver cup challenge worth 10 guineas to kill 50 rats in 7 minutes. Jerry managed it in 4 minutes 49 seconds.

The rat pits were colosseums in miniature, generally circular constructions built from wooden boards with a circumference of around 10 feet (3 metres) and sides several feet deep. This design was intended so the rats could not hide in a corner when a dog was introduced. They were situated in pubs across the country, with at least 70 in London by the middle of the nineteenth century. Defenders of the barbaric practice claimed that it helped reduce the rodent population. The pits in fact did the exact opposite, as landlords were forced to order in weekly deliveries of rats (and even on occasion breed them) in order to supply enough to satisfy the crowds.

The aforementioned James 'Jimmy' Shaw would order in up to 700 rats a week to fill the pit in the parlour of his pub, in which they would be pitted against a dog at up to 50 at a time. Mr Shaw's own dog, Tiny, reputedly once killed 200 rats in an hour. A contemporary painting, *Rat-catching at the 'Blue Anchor' Tavern, Bunhill Row, Finsbury, London*, portrays a rat fight in what was Jimmy Shaw's pub. An all-male crowd of evidently mixed class, gentlemen in evening dress, costermongers in corduroy jackets and a couple of soldiers, watch as a dog tears into rats little smaller than itself. At the edge of the rat pit two piles of rodents have heaved together in defence.

Eventually, growing public disquiet at the treatment of the rats (and dogs) in the pits, as well as wider concerns that breeders were leading to an influx of rat populations in neighbourhoods, forced politicians to outlaw the practice. The last public rat-baiting competition took place in Leicestershire in 1912. The owner of that final rat pit was prosecuted and fined, and another brief but brutal chapter in the long history between humans and rats came to a close.

Try as I might, I have been unable to find any evidence of a surviving rat pit. They were, by their nature, temporary constructions. But I do discover that Jimmy Shaw's pub is still standing, albeit renamed the Artillery Arms. I visited one night to see if there was any evidence of its notorious history but when I chatted to the on-duty manager he had no idea what a rat pit even was and didn't seem all that keen to find out. I stayed for a drink in any case, watching the city workers sipping wine and eating crisps, and imagining the raucous din a few centuries earlier as the rats ran for their lives, roared on by a baying crowd.

Like those marshalling the rat pits, the Victorian rat-catchers were skilful showmen who carefully cultivated both their own public images and those of the rats to boost their business. Reading some contemporary accounts, it appears to me they are more illusionists than anything else, Dickensian snake-charmers who drew upon the public fascination with rats and exploited their fears.

Most prominent among them was Jack Black himself, who wore a costume of white leather breeches, a green coat and a scarlet waistcoat with a gold band looped around his top hat. Across his shoulder he wore a belt bearing rats cast from a plaster mould he made himself from a rodent corpse. For the metal, he used his wife's melted-down saucepans. On the top of every bill he handed to clients was carefully printed 'V. R. rat and mole destroyer to her majesty'.

The chronicler of Victorian street life, Henry Mayhew, was particularly fascinated by Jack Black and conducted a series of interviews with him for his book, *London Labour and the London Poor*. Mayhew's first encounter with him was on Hart Street (near Fenchurch Street station) where he met Black standing on top of his cart painted with rats on the side, surrounded by a gawping crowd. 'Here I saw him dip his hand into this cage of rats and take out as many as he could hold, a feat which generally caused an "oh!" of wonder to escape from the crowd, especially when they observed that his hands were unbitten,' Mayhew observed. 'Men swore the animals had been tamed, as he let them run up his arms like squirrels, and the people gathered round beheld them sitting on his shoulders or cleaning their faces with their front-paws, or rising up on their hind legs like little kangaroos, and sniffing about his ears and cheeks.'

Mayhew later arranged to see Jack Black at his home in Battersea, and came across a very different man from the street performer he had witnessed. He describes his rough, uncombed grey hair, jet-black whiskers and 'an expression of kindliness in his countenance, a quality which does not exactly agree with one's preconceived notion of rat catchers'.

Black's parlour was a Merlin-like treasure trove filled with all manner of natural curiosities. In a caged box he kept a white ferret called Polly. Dotted about the walls were various birds and mammals stuffed by Black, as well as a collection of beetles. Mayhew describes strips of drying fish dangling from the ceiling which, according to Black, he caught by hand from the Thames, eschewing the use of any tackle and merely watching the tides and behaviour of the fish. Up close his white leather breeches were pockmarked with rat bites and scratches, and his hands and face deeply scarred.

Jack Black caught his first rat when he was nine and later used to hunt for them with ferrets around the ponds in Regent's Park. But birds were his earliest love. At 15 he started bird-fancying (another Victorian practice, where songbirds were captured and bred to sell on the streets) and developed a particular infatuation with linnets. Black described to Mayhew in great detail the joyous melody of the bird, insisting 'there are four and twenty changes in a linnet's song'. A keen student of British birdsong, he also described nightingales, hedge and garden warblers, redstarts and blackcaps. 'I have got their sounds in my ear and my mouth,' he told Mayhew. Like the Camden rat-catcher Matthew Blackwell, Black professed a deep, if unconventional, appreciation of nature, which eventually drew him towards rats.

In his late teens, Jack Black started ratting again; this time with a black-and-tan terrier called Billy. His first main contract was working in London's parks, and later in various military barracks across the capital. He paid careful attention to his work, uncovering evidence to better understand the behaviour of his quarry. Clearing out 32 rats from one burrow in Regent's Park he discovered a treasure trove of cached food inside: 'fish, birds and loads of eggs – duck eggs – of every kind.' In another well-to-do household infested with rats he discovered the rodents had carried off 'a great quantity of table napkins and silver spoons and forks' as well as shoes and boots, aprons and pieces of silk. So much had

vanished that the servants in the property had been accused
of theft and discharged.

Black suffered many rat bites over his 35-year career, three
of which nearly killed him. 'When a rat's bite touches the
bone, it makes you faint in a minute, and it bleeds dreadful,'
he told Mayhew. 'Ah, most terrible – just as if you had been
stuck with a penknife.' But he also exacted his own revenge.
According to Mayhew, Black confessed that 'unbeknown to
his wife' he had eaten dead rats. When cooked, he asserted,
they were 'as moist as rabbits, and quite as nice'.

Jack Black also bred rats. A man not known for
understatement, he boasted to Mayhew that he had bred
'the finest collection of pied rats which has ever been
knowed in the world'. He started his breeding programme
from a wild white rat he caught in Hampstead and a black
specimen retrieved from 'Messrs Hodges and Lowman's' in
Regent Street. From that pair, Black produced more than
1,000 descendants of all manner of colours: fawn and white,
black and white, brown and white, red and white, blue-
black, and even black, white and red. Looking at the varied
colours of my rats, Molly and Ermintrude, I wonder if
either of them originally hailed from a Jack Black rat.

I have an appointment with another modern-day rat-
catcher: Craig Morris, who works across Hampshire
alongside his border terrier, also Monty (evidently a popular
name for a ratting dog). The pair have been in business
together for 11 years after Craig first bought Monty as a
family dog. Craig's daughter would dress the puppy up in
outlandish costumes. Now, full-grown, the dog spends his
days hunting rats.

We meet on a residential street in Winchester where Craig has been called out to an infestation in a house belonging to a hoarder. This, he tells me, is not an uncommon job for a rat-catcher. As the elderly woman who owns the house comes out to greet us, I am struck by his sensitivity in dealing with what is evidently a complex psychological disorder. The 53-year-old Craig works with Monty in the same way, calling to him softly and sparingly. 'He's a good companion,' Craig tells me. 'I chat to him all the time. I even share my lunch with him.'

Craig presents me with gloves and overalls and we make our way into the house. The woman has been here a long time but is now moving in with family nearby and her children want to empty the house in order to sell it. They are reluctant to deal with the towering piles of rubbish inside because they are worried they will disturb the rats. That is what we are here to do instead.

Craig had scoped outside the house a few days previously and discovered a large and clearly well-used rat burrow dug next to a drainpipe. Inside, he says, the family had reported stacks of heaped books and clothes moving on their own accord as rats scurried underneath.

Monty, whose fur is brown with grey streaks, offset by a scarlet collar, charges in and we follow close behind. One room is heaped with clothes into which Monty dives as he follows the scent of rats; the next is stacked with floor-to-ceiling piles of books, including the biography of Dickie Bird and every British monarch for the past 500 years, shelves of faded nursery rhymes and anthologies of fairy tales. There are also old newspapers, VHS cassettes and a collection of Japanese dolls stuffed into a glass cabinet.

From here, Monty darts, nose twitching, into the bedroom. The bed, in fact, is not even visible under piles of old blankets, clothes and stuffed toys at least a metre deep. This is where Craig suspects the rats are hiding. Monty pants and sniffs, leaps up and dives down, but is blocked in every direction by the sheer volume of stuff.

As we watch I am tensed, waiting at any moment for a rat (or several) to charge out from their hiding places. Monty, however, shows no fear. Early on in his ratting career he did get bitten, Craig explains, on his face and his chest, but he has since learned the importance of striking first. 'With rats he's just hard-wired to do it,' he says. 'It's in the breeding.'

Monty is thwarted. The rats are too dug in. So instead we head outside and inspect the perimeter of the house. Craig shows me the burrow he previously blocked up with steel wool and several large stones, and appears gratified that it hasn't been disturbed since his last visit. We also inspect a neighbouring property where another pest-control worker has recently been and laid down pellets of shiny blue poison in the open air, where it is freely accessible to any number of birds, small mammals or pets. Craig shakes his head, angry at such a scattergun application of a lethal poison, something he says is far too common.

Originally from Manchester, he started his career working as a gamekeeper in Hampshire and was drawn to the trade because he wanted to work outside. However, he encountered a very different world to what he had envisaged, and in particular a culture of indiscriminate killing of wildlife and the use of traps and poisons, deemed a necessary part of the job. He quit soon afterwards and set up in pest control instead, specialising in rats and moles.

He doesn't use anticoagulant poisons but will on occasion deploy a lethal rodenticide containing a substance called cholecalciferol, which is used to treat vitamin-D deficiency in humans. When ingested by rats it prompts a lethal rise in their blood calcium levels and, after a few days, acute kidney failure. It is available only to those with a licence, and the blocks of poison bait must be used completely covered and with a wire attached to prevent rats dragging them off. While Craig defends it as effective and ethical with little chance of being ingested by other wildlife, some experts are critical of the poison, arguing that it leads to an excruciating death.

Otherwise, Craig relies on typical spring traps with a home-made bait of peanut butter and a fruit and nut mix from his own lunchbox. He loads up about a dozen traps before we make our way back into the house and down into the cellar. Here we find piles of rat poo, some fresher than others, as well as the remains of a magnificent wasp nest covered with intricate curls of paper that reminds me of a barrister's wig.

We set the traps and Craig returns a few days later. When he does, he sends me a photograph of a decent-sized rat whose neck was broken in one of them. Craig reckons it is a juvenile because of its light grey fur but it has clearly already had a tough life, with one eye cloudy and scarred and its tail reduced to a stump.

Craig tells me he and Monty have found themselves in plenty of uncomfortable situations with rats. He has been in domestic properties with such serious infestations that rats are skittering about the work surfaces. Other times he has ventured up into loft spaces with 10 or so rats writhing about. 'Sometimes you go up there and the whole space is just moving,' he tells me. But he insists he has no fear of rats; indeed, quite the opposite. Over the years attempting to outwit them, he has fostered a strong appreciation for their intelligence and adaptability. 'I just think they're amazing,' he says. 'They are just fascinating creatures. They are only dirty because of the conditions we leave around.'

As for Monty, Craig insists, hunting for rats is just another game to him. At the end of a long day the pair return home and the first thing Monty will always do is head straight to his stash of balls and begin chasing them around.

An appreciation, even an affection, for their quarry can be gleaned from the accounts of several nineteenth-century rat-catchers, alongside a considered understanding of their wider place in the ecosystem. Jack Black did employ poisons – he sold his own special batch to customers with the guarantee it would instantly kill – but others eschewed the use of toxins altogether, relying instead on dogs and ferrets.

Ike Matthews, a Victorian rat-catcher in Manchester who in 1898 published a short book detailing his 25-year career, argued: 'I don't believe in poisoning, as one never knows where it ends – the rats being likely to carry the poisoned food about and then dogs, hens, pigs, pigeons, &c., may pick it up.' Even a particularly dramatic 1850 pamphlet entitled *Rat!!!Rat!!!Rat!!! A Treatise on the nature, fecundity and devastating character of the rat and its cruel cost to the nation with the best means for its extermination*, concludes that when it comes to poison, 'the most merciful and speedy way of destroying rats is to let the dogs kill them'.

The early years of the twentieth century eroded any such sensibilities. The third plague pandemic, which erupted from Hong Kong in 1894 and spread across the world, brought with it a new wave of terror. The disease also broke upon European shores, including in Glasgow where in August 1900, 35 people were infected and 16 killed. Only two years earlier the French physician (and eventual chief medical officer) Paul-Louis Simond had proven in laboratory experiments that rat fleas were a vector for the plague. Rats were suddenly identified as public enemy number one.

Researchers at the University of Oslo recently conducted an analysis of the Glasgow plague outbreak which actually somewhat exonerated rats, finding instead that the disease spread through human-to-human transmission among the overcrowded and unsanitary tenements of the city's Gorbals district on the south bank of the river Clyde. The Oslo study examined old local authority records of the outbreak and found that while a significant number of rats were trapped in the neighbourhoods where plague was present, not a single one bore any trace of the disease. Not that it mattered. In Britain, the US and a host of other countries a new objective had been declared in the millennia-old war on rats: outright extermination, by any means possible.

In 1908, the first ever 'rat destruction bill' was introduced to the House of Commons by the Liberal politician Charles McLaren MP (later Lord Aberconway). A wealthy industrialist and landowner who had started his career in journalism, McLaren knew how to spin a story. He told his fellow MPs that Britain's population of rats was equivalent to the human population (around 40 million at the time) and the annual loss of food spoiled or stolen by rats was £69 million (nearly £1 billion in today's money). That figure, McLaren insisted, equated to 1,864,235,290 bottles of Bass beer, 2,640,000,000 loaves of bread, 44,000,000 tonnes of coal or enough money to keep one large hospital running for 500 years.

After taking his seat in the Lords, McLaren played an integral role in the formation of the Vermin Repression Society in 1919. Based at 44 Bedford Row in London, the society represented a host of wealthy landowners and had access to the highest corridors of power, where they lobbied government. Another member, Lord Lambourne, called in 1920 for a 'crusade against rats to be carried out along national lines'.

The same year the society formed, the government passed the Rats and Mice (Destruction) Act, on 23 December 1919. The act placed a legal obligation on every private individual to destroy rodents and deal with any infestation on land or property they owned, or face a fine of £5. The act also called for the enforcement to be carried out by every local authority in the country. This marked a major escalation in rodent control. In the ports and streets, the sewers and sludge ships, Britain declared all-out war.

The Vermin Repression Society celebrated the passing of the act in typical style, with a private dinner for its assorted luminaries at the Connaught Rooms in London. Its chairman, Alfred E. Moore, later published a short pamphlet entitled *The Rat, man's implacable foe and a nation's economic burden*, which sought to illustrate the methods and means to eradicate rats from the earth. Moore described it as 'the sacred duty of every living one of us to take his or her place in the world war against these living emblems of depredation, filth and disease and to destroy ruthlessly every rat or mouse on every possible occasion'. Without enduring, coordinated and ordered effort, he warned, 'there is in my opinion a danger that future generations may easily see the wellbeing of mankind seriously menaced by uncountable rat hordes.'

Rat-catchers and their dogs were no longer enough. The Vermin Repression Society discussed deploying the Boy Scouts nationwide and even considered a proposal emanating from a 'professor of hygiene' in Germany to deliberately circulate a virus among rat populations, which he assured was not harmful to people. Even given the febrile atmosphere of the time, this was ultimately deemed a step too far. But Moore championed pretty much any other method of rat disposal. In his pamphlet he suggests flooding rat burrows with tar and beating any escapees to death with sticks, and using a 'strong lithographic varnish spread' on surfaces used by rats (a prototype of modern-day glue traps). He also goes into considerable detail on the efficacy of poisons. Among the lethal (to humans as well as rats) toxins he recommends for use are arsenic, strychnine, phosphorous and barium carbonate.

He cites promising results obtained from Venice where an elevator containing 25,000 tonnes of grain was fumigated with hydrocyanic acid gas, although concedes the risk to human health is probably too great. Not so fumigating hedgerows with high-strength sulphur dioxide gas, a method he praises for its efficacy in eliminating adult rats as well as their pups.

Moore even suggests several lethal recipes including oatmeal mixed with sugar, grated parmesan cheese and 'a small quantity of strychnine', and a dish of chicken's heads laced with poison. 'Put a pinch of strychnine into each neck and dip in blood,' Moore advises. 'The brain is such a tempting morsel no rat can withstand it.'

For a time, the citizens of the twentieth century believed they really could finally rid themselves of the rat. During the Second World War, the Women's Land Army was mobilised to dispatch any rat they could find across the nation's farms, including pumping Cymag (a now-banned cyanide gas) into burrows. The slogan the authorities adopted was: 'Kill that rat: it's doing Hitler's work.'

In 1949, Britain's Rats and Mice Destruction Act was updated to grant additional powers and responsibilities on local government to enforce rodent control. But the rats had the advantage of any guerrilla army: an ability to launch nocturnal raids and retreat into secret burrows, a shared intelligence network and a hugely effective spying operation, combined with an indefatigable ability to adapt and survive.

As the decades passed, it became increasingly apparent that the war on rats was doomed to fail. The rodents coped with whatever people threw at them. Meanwhile, improved sanitation and housing reduced the risk of disease transmission. As the dystopian carnage predicted by the likes of Alfred Moore and Charles McLaren failed to materialise, both the political and public appetite waned. Total eradication became tempered with talk of 'control'. The rules of engagement were once more rewritten for the uneasy and uncertain relationship with rats, one which persists today. Even if there is now a (slightly) greater tolerance, I wonder to what extent the twentieth-century approach to rat extermination still underpins our cultural awareness of rats.

Somewhere along the way over the past century, the traditional rat-catcher fell by the wayside. The ancient trade became rebranded 'pest control', with giant companies such as Rentokil cornering the market. Rentokil has an experimental facility on the outskirts of London it calls an 'innovation centre', where the firm trials the latest scientific methods to dispose of and deter rats. In January 2023, it announced it was developing new facial-recognition surveillance technology in partnership with Vodafone to track rat infestations and feed back real-time analysis to a central command centre, which can decide how best to dispose of the rat.

There is also work taking place to assess the potential of genetic engineering to render rats infertile (a technique already employed in mosquitos). In 2017, researchers at Edinburgh's Roslin Institute announced they were investigating the feasibility of releasing genetically modified male rats with an 'x-shredder' code inserted into their DNA, meaning they could only ever pass on the y chromosome and never have female pups. In time, therefore, the population would decline; possibly catastrophically so.

In November 2022, researchers at Adelaide University progressed this concept by announcing the results of a study into causing infertility in female laboratory mice. Using computer modelling, the researchers found that introducing 250 mice, whose genetics had been modified with something called t-CRISPR, which alters a female's fertility gene, into an island population of 200,000 rodents could wipe them out within 20 years.

Such technology remains theoretical, but it could eventually equip humanity with the ability to eradicate rats, a process which has preoccupied civilisations for many thousands of years, dating back to the time when cats were a cosseted species in Ancient Egypt, in part because of their lethal ability to kill rats. It also poses a minefield of ethical questions. Rats may prove destructive in the environment but they are also a vital food source for other animals. If we remove them from the food chain, who knows what the knock-on effects would be?

There is also the question of where this all leads. After the successful deployment of the technology against mosquitos, and if the rat is ultimately expunged, would other unpopular species, such as the urban fox or carrion crow, follow? And above all, in the midst of an extinction and biodiversity crisis caused by human activity, what right do we have to deem which animal is permitted to share the earth with us, and which is not?

CHAPTER SEVEN

Prey

I was strolling along the Morecambe seafront when I first came upon *The Rats*. I had been visiting the Lancashire seaside town on the weekend of the Queen's Platinum Jubilee to write an article on an attempted record-breaking celebratory lunch being held along its promenade. After interviewing various civic dignitaries and a few of the locals involved, I took a walk up to the old Victorian clock tower that marks the spot where, before it burned down in the 1980s, the central pier used to stretch out over the quicksilver sands of Morecambe Bay.

Nearby, past a few shuttered-up shops and a derelict pub, I noticed the Old Pier Bookshop. It occupied a corner spot at the end of a row of sandstone buildings with *BOOKS* stamped in black on the peeling paint of its side wall. Walking in I was struck by that heady, familiar and comforting smell of ink, paper and dust. Books filled every available corner, stacked floor to ceiling as if the walls themselves were constructed out of them. Narrow passages snaked between towering shelves with seemingly no discernible order: old botany guides alongside obscure cricket almanacs and detective novels. One online review I later read describes the Old Pier as like someone has taken James Joyce's famously impenetrable *Finnegans Wake* and turned it into a bookshop.

Owner Tony Vettese has run the place for decades. With a shock of black hair and wearing a checked shirt and waistcoat, Tony seemingly has a book for every topic of conversation, and every customer. In between chatting he constantly darted off to fulfil requests for books, which miraculously he produces from the clutter. To assist with my article about the Queen he disappeared into another hidden corridor before emerging with old books and souvenir magazines published to mark previous jubilees and royal weddings. When I told him I was writing a book about rats, he mouthed the words 'James Herbert' before disappearing once more into the bowels of his shop. As I waited, I studied the cover of a heavy hardback 1970s guide to the flora and fauna of Lancashire, teetering alarmingly above my head.

The book he returned with was *Domain*, the third in the spectacularly successful trilogy written by James Herbert who, before his death at the age of 69 in 2013, was Britain's bestselling horror writer. His first novel, *The Rats*, was published in 1974 and depicted a London overrun by mutant flesh-eating rodents. He followed this up with *Lair*, published a few years later, in which the rats had relocated to Epping Forest on the outskirts of East London to plot their return.

In the final book in the trilogy, *Domain*, published in 1984, London is in the aftermath of nuclear war and the rats have once more risen up from the sewers. Tony Vettese pressed the book into my hands, a pair of gleaming red rat eyes staring out from the otherwise black cover, and urged me to read it. Sometime later I realised he never actually asked for any money for the book. I try to ring the shop several times over the following months to pay him back, but he never picks up. I still owe him for the book.

James Herbert wrote about London and its rats because that is what he knew best. Born in 1943, he grew up in Aldgate East in the city's docklands, an area largely reduced to rubble by Luftwaffe bombers in the Second World War. His parents were market traders who ran a fruit and veg stall seven days a week (later taken on by his brother). They lived in a condemned Victorian block on Whitechapel's Petticoat Lane next to a plot of land where their fellow market traders dumped rotting fruit and vegetables at the end of each day. The sounds that haunted Herbert's childhood were mewing stray cats, which he once described as like 'weeping children', and large rats slithering through the city's wastelands.

Herbert's books were lampooned in the literary press, famously so by Martin Amis in *The Observer* who, writing under his pseudonym, Henry Tilney, described the horror it portrayed as 'enough to make a rodent retch'. And yet, they evidently still tapped into a public fascination. *The Rats* alone sold more than a million copies.

Herbert imagined his nightmarish rodents as the offspring of a failed biology experiment after a rogue zoologist interbred native black rats with another mutant species retrieved from an island in the South Pacific, which had survived nuclear experiments. Having broken out of the laboratory, this new breed proliferated across London, developing a taste for human flesh along the way. In *Domain*, the rats rise up after five nuclear warheads have mushroomed across the capital, unaffected by the radiation that has decimated the human population.

The increasingly ludicrous attempts Herbert's characters concoct to control the ravenous horde – gas, a man-made virus and ultrasonic machines to disrupt their communication frequencies – are not all that dissimilar from some of the proposals put forward by the likes of the Vermin Repression Society. His books exemplify how often our understanding of rats is reduced to this polarised view of us versus them. And also how rats ultimately drive humans to madness.

Rats offer such fertile breeding grounds for horror stories because we see in them a darker reflection of our own society, one that exists below ground and outside of the trappings of civilisation. Writing in the 1930s, the US epidemiologist Hans Zinsser highlighted rats as humanity's closest accomplice in our joint destruction of worlds. Spreading together across the earth, laying waste to landscapes and yet ultimately unable to wipe one another out, Zinsser wrote that 'neither of them is of the slightest earthly use to any other species of living things'.

But can it really be true that rats serve no purpose other than to destroy? This binary approach informs the way we often think of rats. It is rare, in my opinion, that we consider rats as part of a wider ecosystem and the role they play in the food chain. Modern naturalists are as guilty of this as anyone. When we talk and write about wildlife around us, rats very rarely get a look-in. Why no mention of the rats that skulk at the bottom of bird feeders or squirm through the gaps in garden fences we are encouraged to leave for hedgehogs? Why are we told nothing about rats on information boards in nature reserves, when they are a vital food source for birds of prey?

I remember one trip to the RSPB sanctuary at London's Rainham Marshes on the banks of the Thames, where I surprised a huge rat with ginger-hued fur gorging itself on a bird feeder. Oddly, it was my most memorable sighting of the day; a creature that offered a glimpse of Rainham's fascinating history as the dumping ground of the capital before it was allowed to be reclaimed by nature.

For good or ill, they thrive alongside the kingfishers, otters and herons but do not fit into the bucolic image of British wildlife that some like to project. The rats are excluded.

But this is also their world. And our refusal to acknowledge that they exist, other than through our own efforts to eradicate them, means their presence remains relatively unexplored. What do they eat (aside from the food left by humans)? What eats them and in what quantity? And how do our attempts to control rats, in particular the varied poisons we lay down, disrupt the wider ecosystem of which they form an important part?

Later that same summer, I received a message from a friend out of the blue. On the farm where he works they had discovered the sloughed skin of a large grass snake in the compost bins where rats nest. They suspected the snake had moved in to start feeding on the baby rats. Maybe, he wondered, I might like to come and take a look?

Sheffield's Moss Valley sits atop a hidden corner of the city. I had lived here for half a decade before I even knew it existed. The river Moss, which runs along the southern outskirts of Sheffield, provides a natural barrier to this wild, riverine landscape surrounding its tributaries. No roads run all the way through and only a scattering of farms are dotted about. The entirety of the Moss Valley contains some 280 hectares of woodland, around half of which is designated ancient semi-natural woodland. Stately sycamores, beech and oaks, which were coppiced in the post-medieval period before being left to mature in the Victorian era, now blossom across the undulating valley.

For many centuries, the Moss Valley has been used for farming. Old lanes and packhorse routes thread between ancient hedgerows and ditches. In the modern era the valley has become home to a cluster of Sheffield's regenerative farming projects, growing food for sale in the city below.

My friend Mikk Murray works for one of these projects, Moss Valley Market Garden, one of four independent businesses growing food, fruit and flowers, who rent a plot of land and share communal facilities. They have been in existence for 10 years, operating a fruit and vegetable box scheme to around 200 customers, and take a biodynamic and organic approach to farming, one that aims to work with the surrounding wildlife and the rhythms of the land.

I first met Mikk during lockdown when he offered to help with a tree-planting group I was part of. An artist and passionate talker and thinker about landscapes, wildlife and food, he is someone who inspires with his intimate and thoughtful connection to the land. Upon receiving his message about the snakeskin, I head up to

Moss Valley after work one day to meet him, and their hungry snakes.

I arrive when Mikk and the team are packing up the latest batch of boxes for delivery. As they work, they chat about their various struggles with rats over the years. The founder of the business, Martin Bradshaw, tells me that in the past the rats have decimated beetroot beds, skinned grapes off vines and broken into polytunnels in search of sustenance. They also have a particular weakness for squash. The rats will burrow in through the flesh only to steal the seeds from the middle. If left unchecked, he warns, they will easily munch through three-quarters of a crop.

They operate rat-control measures here which I have become increasingly convinced over the course of writing this book are the most effective – and environmentally friendly – approach to take. Generally, they do nothing, but on occasions when the rat population rapidly spirals they use targeted control measures, either through hiring in a person with a rifle to shoot them or placing spring-loaded traps in polytunnels. They have reduced opportunities for rodents wherever they can by rat-proofing their farm buildings, and above all have tried to encourage a healthy ecosystem, where as many potential predators as possible can help naturally keep rats in check. That is where the snakes come in, but we will get on to those in due course.

'I just see them as another part of nature really,' Martin says of the farm's resident stowaways. 'Obviously we are taught to have that natural aversion to rats but I don't feel that way towards them. We look at what we can do that is in keeping with a wider respect for nature. We are not going to go out of our way to kill them, but if they cause a nuisance we will trap appropriately.'

In recent years, they say this approach has kept populations in check to the extent where it is quite rare to encounter a rat, during the day at least. One of the most recent rats knocking about the farm, Mikk tells me, they christened 'Mad Max' and adopted as something of a mascot. Mikk first met Max while having a pee in the compost heap. He noticed the rat staring at him, a nasty gash on the side of its face, having presumably just survived an encounter with one of the many predators lurking on the farm. Over the following weeks, Mikk and a few others kept watch over Mad Max, regularly heading out to the compost heap to check he was still alive. Eventually, he disappeared. The Moss Valley, evidently, is a tough place to be a rat.

The orders complete, we take a walk across the farm. Mikk points out several large ponds they have dug in recent years; they contain rafts of floating vegetation, habitats they think first attracted the grass snakes, who feast on amphibians and other small mammals. It is a hot evening in September and I watch crane flies hatching in the long grass surrounding the ponds and dragonflies droning across the water.

We head up past polytunnels containing tomato plants (where they hang wind chimes to deter wildlife and promote better growth) and an orchard heaving with apples. Mikk points out the ancient oaks swirled with ivy and laden with acorns, which inspire some of his paintings. It is early in the season but such is the bountiful crop on the trees that he suspects it may be a mast year (an event occurring every few years when certain trees and shrubs produce a particular abundance of nuts and fruits).

As we stop to munch apples and inspect some of the hedgerows and native trees they have planted as windbreaks around the farm, a hare explodes out of a mature copse a hundred or so metres away. 'You know when you said there are no roads up here,' Mikk says as we watch it bound away. 'There are. Just not the roads we think about. Those hedgerows and ponds are used constantly all day long. And we are just unaware.'

This is the secret world he and his colleagues on the farm have hoped to rely upon to help control the rats. He points out wooden boxes they have installed high up on some of the oldest oaks, which house barn and tawny owls. A neighbouring farm has even installed large wooden raptor poles to encourage buzzards and sparrowhawks to perch and scan for prey. As we speak, a pair of buzzards swirls through the blue sky above us. Foxes also stalk the fields and a mature heron has taken to staking out their new ponds. If you wonder whether a wise and stately heron might think better of eating a rat, then have a look at the many amateur videos taken in urban parks circulating online (but possibly not while eating lunch yourself). The birds will happily gulp them down whole, tail and all.

As well as questioning what else might eat rats, Mikk is increasingly curious about how rodents might predate upon the pests that target their own crops. 'I'm intrigued by what they are up to and what they are doing,' he says of the rats. 'I see them as part of the ecosystem. Are they eating slugs and other pests we don't like, and what is eating them in return?'

He believes that when it comes to rats, we all have a voice in our head warning us their presence heralds disease and possible famine. It is a hostility we all grow up with, one rich in cultural memory. After all, he admits, if he was working on the land in the Moss Valley centuries ago when the annual harvest was a matter of life and death, he too would probably seek to eradicate every rat in sight.

But our world has changed and nowadays he seeks to view that internal voice for what it is: the opinions of others. 'I try to see rats as another thing that we live with,' he says. 'More of a neighbour.'

Which brings us on to the snakes. Searching through the compost heap he built himself out of wooden pallets and fence posts, Mikk produces another freshly discovered piece of snakeskin with glee. I run my fingers along the dry, honeycomb bubbles and breathe in its warm, hessian smell. When they discovered the first skin earlier this summer, they were all so excited they downed tools for half an hour to cluster round the compost heap.

After my visit I consult with various herpetologists about the extent to which rats might form part of a snake's diet. The general consensus is that, despite growing more than a metre in length, grass snakes prefer smaller and easier-to-catch prey such as amphibians. They are, however, known on occasion to snack on small mammals, such as mice and voles, when the chance arises. A full-grown rat, therefore, would probably be out of the question, but their babies, such as those found in the compost heaps of the Moss Valley, would provide a tempting meal.

Elsewhere in the UK, other species of snake are taking advantage of rat populations to extend their range. Along London's Regent's Canal (where I visited with rat-catcher Matthew Blackwell and his ratting dogs), a population of Aesculapian snakes has become established. The non-native snakes, which can grow to two metres long and are skilful climbers, are also known as rat snakes, given their predilection for rodents. Another colony of the snakes has become established in Colwyn Bay in north Wales.

The benign experience of Mikk and his fellow Moss Valley farmers in dealing with rats is not, it is fair to say, a typical one. I have met with farmers who grow crops and rear livestock more intensively and who speak of being deluged by rats as a result. On one memorable occasion I was given a tour of the estate of an extremely rich and well-connected aristocratic landowner in southern England (whom I shall keep anonymous). As we bounced over the fields in his Range Rover, he boasted to me that some years his estate workers had killed in the region of 2,000 rats. That day he also showed me the wire snares they used to kill foxes who encroached on the land (something that remains legal so long as they are designated free-running snares, which relax when the animal stops struggling). He had invited me to inspect his field margins, which he had enlarged and planted with wildflowers, and he spoke with pride of the diverse plants now blossoming and how the increased invertebrate biodiversity had helped to mitigate other pests in his crops. And yet he didn't seem to extend that same logic to dealing with rats and their predators.

Back in 2015, while searching the archives of the Museum of English Rural Life for methods of rat control used on farms over the nineteenth and twentieth centuries, Karen Sayer, a history professor at Leeds University, made some interesting discoveries. Among the various methods of rat disposal she uncovered at the Reading-based museum was an extra-large tin of glue branded 'Ratsticker', manufactured in 1920 by B. Winstone & Sons of Shoe Lane in London, and billed as a 'non-poisonous rat catching compound' that would cause the hapless rodents to die solely of shock.

The rats would soon face far worse. Following the global ramping up of food production that followed the Second

World War, chemical controls increasingly came to the fore. This was the birth of the 'Silent Spring', which Rachel Carson famously warned about in the early 1960s. Synthetic compounds such as Dichlorodiphenyltrichloroethane (DDT) ravaged natural predators and precipitated a collapse in biodiversity across increasingly homogenised landscapes designed to maximise yields at the expense of everything else.

During this new chemical age, specialist poisons were also concocted to counter the rise of the rodents, which, unlike other less adaptable animals, could rapidly flourish across the monocultures created by industrial farming. Indeed, with no other predators around to speak of, they could thrive.

As a result, yet more poisons were laid. The newly developed anticoagulant warfarin, for example, was so liberally applied across British farms that, as Karen Sayer pointed out in a subsequent article for the *British Journal for the History of Science*, by the late 1960s and early 1970s, resistance had started to be discovered in rats. A recent survey conducted by the Campaign for Responsible Rodenticide Use UK claimed genes demonstrating resistance to anticoagulant rodenticide had been detected in 78 per cent of rats.

As the poisons became commonplace, other natural predators higher up in the food chain started increasingly falling victim, either through consuming the bait themselves or by eating stricken rats. These rodenticides work by thinning the blood of rats until they suffer internal haemorrhages and die. Often they can limp on for several days, making them susceptible to predation and causing secondary poisoning.

Despite their wider impact, a second-generation of even more powerful anticoagulant rodenticides soon came to market, around 100 to 1,000 times more toxic than warfarin and other first-generation compounds. Five of these poisons are currently authorised for use in Britain: difenacoum, bromadiolone, brodifacoum, flocoumafen and difethialone.

In 2022, researchers at the UK Centre for Ecology & Hydrology, which is responsible for the Predatory Bird Monitoring Scheme (a national programme measuring the presence of contaminants in the livers of birds of prey), published the sixth in a series of annual reports, investigating the prevalence of secondary poisoning in barn owls. Out of 100 carcasses examined in the study, 88 per cent contained traces of second-generation anticoagulants, a level that has remained broadly similar over the past six years, despite efforts to introduce greater stewardship of the poisons. There remains little research showing a clear link between these sub-lethal doses and an adverse effect on barn owl populations, but the likes of the Barn Owl Trust argue that rodenticides are almost certainly a significant cause of barn owl decline and remain an issue of serious concern for a host of other species.

It is not just animals that directly predate rodents that end up consuming the poisons. A 2010 study examining first- and second-generation anticoagulants contained within British hedgehogs (the first to analyse the impact of rodenticide on non-target insectivores) found 66.7 per cent of 120 animals tested contained residues of the poisons. By proving the presence of this toxicity in an animal that does not even eat rats, this study confirmed the extent to which the poisons leached into ecosystems.

Occasionally, even apex predators fall victim. In January 2022, a satellite-tagged white-tailed eagle, which had been released as part of a reintroduction project on the Isle of Wight, was discovered dead in North Dorset. Subsequent toxicology reports found the young eagle had ingested 7 times the lethal dose of the second-generation anticoagulant brodifacoum. The bird was discovered on a shooting estate and was one of four white-tailed eagles released in the programme to have died or suffered a suspected poisoning along the south coast of England in a matter of months. A subsequent police review of the death ruled that there was 'insufficient evidence to prove an offence of wilful poisoning by an individual', although campaigners have long suspected foul play. Either way it demonstrates the prevalence – and lethal properties of these chemicals – and how their reach extends well beyond rats.

Prior to this avalanche of chemicals, rat-catching was far more of an art form, one which utilised predators and a greater understanding of rat behaviour. Professor Karen Sayer points out one study, conducted by the ecologist Charles Elton and published in the *British Journal of Animal Behaviour*, on the potential of cats to manage rural rat populations. Elton analysed field studies carried out during the Second World War under the auspices of the Agricultural Research Council, which counted the prevalence of cats and rats across various mixed livestock farms. In the right circumstances and with cats fed just enough to keep them anchored to farms but not so much that it would put them off hunting, Elton concluded cats could be effective within a localised vicinity and a lethal weapon in the war on rats.

On a foggy night in Thixendale, North Yorkshire, I chance upon a few of these expert ratters myself. I am lost, driving along a country track peering through the windscreen into near total darkness, when I come across a farmhouse and stop to ask for directions. I am looking for a man called Robert, with whom I have made an appointment to talk about rats. Confusingly, a different man called Robert opens the door, and when I tell him who I am looking for and why, he immediately starts telling me his own rat stories. His two cats, one ginger, one black, mew on the doorstep. Their faces are badly scarred from years of rat-catching on his farm. The ginger one is missing an eye.

His farm, he tells me, is plagued by rats and for years he and his cats have been devoted to driving them out. Over the many nights hunting them he has been left highly impressed by the intelligence of the rodents. He tells me how the farm rats were able to establish when he would be coming out to shoot them and therefore scatter in advance. Typically, he would meet up with a friend at 10 p.m. to head towards a nearby rat-infested barn, but after a few occasions they noticed that by the time they arrived the rodents had already vanished. They then adjusted their arrival time to two hours later and discovered the barn teeming with rats once more.

A recent study by researchers at the Institute of Psychology of the Polish Academy of Sciences in Warsaw, published in *Nature*, explored the extent to which rats possess an innate understanding of the passage of time. The research team trained 16 rats to press a lever for exactly 3.2 seconds in order to receive food. Over the course of training, the rats demonstrated an ability to learn from previous mistakes and improve their timing to perfect the lever press and ensure maximum reward. It may sound trivial, but this discovery reveals a complex cognitive ability, previously only presumed to exist in humans and primates. Lead author of the study team, Dr Tadeusz Konowicz, later told the *New Scientist* magazine that at first they couldn't believe the results. 'We were even thinking, are the rats somehow tricking us?' he said.

Back in Thixendale, I leave one Robert and, with the benefit of his directions, head back along the farm track to find the other. Eventually I come across the home of Robert Fuller, one of Britain's leading wildlife artists and maker of documentary films. When I arrive, it is long after dinner-time but he is still pottering about in his gallery and adjoining oak-beamed studio. He greets me warmly and takes me on an impromptu tour of the previously derelict farmhouse he and his wife Victoria have transformed.

Here in acrylic and oil he documents the wildlife of the surrounding valleys, and more exotic climes. He shows me a painting he is currently working on of a black bear he recently encountered in Alaska. There are also portraits of weasels and stoats, whose local dynasties he has followed more closely, he believes, than any other film-maker in the world. Has he ever painted a rat, I wonder, scanning the many animals adorning the gallery walls. 'Oh no,' he shudders. 'I can be near any other animal, but not rats.'

Born in Great Givendale on the other side of the A166 and a few miles away from his current home in Thixendale, where he moved in 1998, Robert has a deep love for this landscape and (rats aside) the creatures residing within it. It was an obsession that started when he was a young boy growing up on the family farm. Among his earliest memories are staring into the garden pond for hours on end, so engrossed that when his mum was mowing the lawn she had to lift up his legs to cut the grass underneath. As he peered into the water he watched an aquatic world of incredible complexity unfolding before him: the larvae of great diving beetles catching tadpoles and sucking out the insides, dragonfly larvae and water nymphs, pea clams and water fleas. 'My mum thought there was something wrong with me,' he grins. 'And maybe there was.'

What he describes as a largely 'feral' upbringing roaming the hills collided with the drudgery and brutality of his local comprehensive school. Robert experiences severe dyslexia, a condition either misunderstood or ignored by his teachers, who treated his inability to read and write as an act of wilful disobedience. During RE lessons every week the teacher would make him read the Bible aloud to the class, no matter how many times he faltered over the words. In the end Robert simply started skipping class, preferring to go fishing in a local stream with a friend instead. By the time he left he remained unable to read the whole alphabet, although he had already started to demonstrate a unique skill for drawing and painting, selling his work to surrounding farms.

He secured a place studying art at York Technical College, and later, wildlife illustration in Carmarthen in south Wales. Aged 20, he started working as a professional wildlife artist and over the ensuing three decades has never stopped. Intimacy is key to Robert Fuller's work and his approach has never changed. He spends endless hours in the field monitoring the wildlife he draws and paints and has constructed ideal habitats to encourage animals to settle and make them easier to observe.

Around a decade ago, however, he grew frustrated. While creatures such as kestrel and barn owl had occupied nesting locations he had built for them, when night fell or they disappeared inside he lost sight. To explore these largely hidden worlds he started investing in wildlife cameras and now possesses an array of 120 or so, which he has persuaded neighbouring landowners to erect across the valley. All the footage feeds into a dozen screens in a dedicated room in their house, which he and Victoria continually monitor. As we sit on two office chairs with a cup of tea it is like a wildlife mission control, with a barn owl preening itself on one screen and a kestrel perched for the night on another.

Robert points out a screen that displays a large rat having clambered up a tree to feast on some feed he has put out for buzzards. We watch the well-fed rodent, whose eyes shine like black marbles on the camera night-vision display, preening itself and smoothing its fur and whiskers as it eats. He may not like them, but installing so many cameras across the landscape has provided Robert with an insight into the secret lives of rats which few people possess.

As well as exploring the wildlife of Thixendale in his youth, Robert Fuller was also committed to eliminating its rats. Back then, he explains, local farmers would periodically come together to join forces against a cluster of rats in a particular area. He says they would gather with their terriers and rabbit-net any escape routes before turning over infested hay bales and setting the dogs free. I have read about these country meet-ups in several old books. They called them 'rat wars'.

'It's grim thinking about it now as someone who is a total wildlife conservationist, but that would have been seen as enjoyment in a way,' he admits. 'We used to catch hundreds some days, but the old boys used to catch thousands.' Occasionally, Robert was nipped by a rat during these purges but says he has never been badly bitten, although he did once have one bolt up his trouser leg and end up clambering around his neck like a furious, thrashing scarf. There are other rat stories that farmers in Thixendale tell of the rodents attacking babies. When Robert and Victoria first moved into their derelict farmhouse they were warned, Victoria recalls, to keep their infant daughter safe.

In his twenties, Robert started to gain a greater understanding of the other animals that might predate rats. Back then he kept a female goshawk who was particularly skilled at hunting them. 'She would always try and take out another predator,' he explains. In recent years his cameras have picked up some remarkable attacks upon rats by goshawks, tawny and barn owls and buzzards, as well as the occasional fox trying its luck. He plays me some of the recordings of the raptors ghosting over the unsuspecting rat before tearing down upon it.

And, in turn, he has witnessed up close the varied diet of the rats. He shows me footage of rats attacking a pair of mating toads (ignoring the toxic chemicals secreted from their skin to ward off predators), harvesting snails as food caches, and rolling away eggs to feast upon. He has watched rats take out a bird nest on many occasions and work together to kill larger mammals such as rabbits. 'I see them almost like hyenas in a way,' he says. 'They are underestimated in how they work together in a pack, and rats are the same.'

Rats, he admits, are 'astonishing things', albeit animals that send a shiver down his spine. 'They are one of the most successful mammals in the world, without a shadow of doubt. It's incredible what they can do, where they can live and what they can live off.'

Above all, it is their pitched battles with the local weasels and stoats that have amazed Robert. Watching the tactics and savagery deployed by both the rodents and mustelids is, he says, as captivating as any predator hunting in the Serengeti. 'I try to explain to people that I've seen cheetahs take down Thomson's gazelles [an antelope that can sprint up to 55mph and is the fourth-fastest land animal on earth] but this is every bit as spectacular and probably even much rarer for someone to witness,' he says.

In 2014, Robert started monitoring the weasels living on his land. He always had an interest in mustelids and kept ferrets in his youth. When he started recording their behaviour, he freely admits that it turned into an unhealthy obsession. It started with a sole female weasel he noticed passing through his garden. He started putting food out for her, dead mice tied to a falconry bell in his studio that would tinkle whenever she ate them. He then built her a nest, taking a hawthorn stump, filling it with dry grass and placing a camera on top. Eventually she moved in and had her first litter of kits. Before long, the rats and stoats also got wind of her secret spot.

To deter predators, Robert says, the weasel embarked on a pre-emptive strike, leading her litter of kits to a nearby rat nest, where they attacked and killed the young. But it did not keep her enemies at bay for long. A while later, Robert discovered her limping and bleeding. He suspected a stoat rather than a rat had attacked her by the bite marks – the former clamp and twist their jaws while rats tend to slash with their teeth.

She survived, but the stoat (slightly larger than a weasel) returned every single day, attempting to kill her and her seven young kits. Robert came to her aid, rebuilding the nest with the injured weasel still inside and tossing her lumps of chicken leg whenever she came out to screech a complaint at the intrusion. He meshed every possible entrance apart from two tiny weasel-shaped holes. It worked, for a spell, until eventually the stoat managed to kill her. Two of her kits also succumbed, but five survived.

The following year, Robert resolved to pursue the stoat instead. For the next three seasons he tracked every move of the stoat, whom he nicknamed White Muzzle, missing family weddings, birthdays and other celebrations. 'I became the first person to film wild weasels and stoats in their nest with kits,' he tells me of his films, which have appeared on nature programmes including a *BBC Natural World* documentary. 'There is no one else as daft as me.'

Robert no longer hunts with his beloved terriers, which tangle about our feet as we talk, but he still kills rats. He estimates he shoots several hundred a year attempting to sneak onto his garden bird feeders, and uses them in turn as meat to lure in raptors to observe. He stresses that despite his dislike for rats and the destruction they cause, he would never lay down poison of any sort to kill them.

'Secondary poisoning is massive for birds of prey,' he tells me. He has held barn owls which have ingested so much anticoagulant that an electric-blue discharge drains out of them as they bleed out. He has known of badgers and dogs dying after snuffling up even a small amount of toxic pellets. He has also witnessed red kites and buzzards die from rodenticide. In the past he has found dead mice and opened them up and found their insides stained blue with poison.

On one level Robert Fuller's war on rats continues. He believes the damage they pose to the wildlife he painstakingly documents is far too severe for the rodents to be left unchecked. When I point out that weasels and stoats are similarly renowned for plundering bird nests, he asks me which I would rather have in my garden – a family of weasels or 200 rats?

That is a choice far too many landowners prefer not to even bother making. By carpeting the land in toxic rodenticide, predators from rodents to mustelids to birds of prey can all fall victim. Robert Fuller is no defender of rats but like any naturalist knows that the idea of 'us and them' disregards the complexity of natural ecosystems. This is the nature he sees, one in which owls pounce, rats hunt in packs, and stoats and weasels kill each other's young. These are savage, bloody, but wonderfully intricate worlds that humans terminally alter with our drip-feed of poison.

Increasing concerns over secondary poisoning are beginning to belatedly force authorities into action. In 2022, the Canadian province of British Columbia introduced a permanent ban on the sale and use of second-generation anticoagulants, with only a few 'essential' sectors such as healthcare and food production permitted to still utilise them. In the Netherlands, the government has removed anticoagulant rodenticide for public use, with other countries expected to follow suit. By the end of 2024 in the UK, it will be illegal to use two second-generation anticoagulant rodenticides – bromadiolone and difenacoum – unless associated with a building. The pest control industry has previously agreed to restrict the use of the other three second-generation anticoagulants to areas in and around buildings. The latest ban would effectively render all second-generation anticoagulants illegal for open use. Campaigners hope that this can finally restrict the extent of poisons leaching into the environment and further impacting on wildlife.

For the rats, I suppose, it marks another small victory in their ongoing battle for survival in the face of whatever humanity throws at them.

CHAPTER EIGHT

Borders

There are four border markers in Lloydminster, Alberta. The 100-foot red steel columns tower above six lanes of motorway traffic, separating the intersection of highways 16 and 17, city hall and a branch of KFC. In this small Canadian frontier city of low-rise shopping malls and gas station forecourts, the markers are proudly regarded as the largest in the world.

They stand on the boundary of the third and fourth meridian, the invisible lines established by nineteenth-century colonists in their surveys as they journeyed across North America, and whose maps denoting the land they claimed left Lloydminster neatly split in two. The western side of the city belongs to Alberta and the eastern half to the neighbouring province of Saskatchewan.

The border markers are intended to represent a potted history of this huge sweep of prairie land. One stands for its original inhabitants, the First Nations and Métis, and another the 2,600 or so Barr Colonists, led by the English clergymen George Exton Lloyd and Isaac Montgomery Barr, who emigrated in the early twentieth century as part of a wave of settlers displacing these Indigenous communities. A third pillar represents the agricultural boom that followed as the settlers felled the virgin forests to carve out space for their cattle herds. And the last represents the oil and gas industry that has driven the economy in more recent decades.

Perhaps one day they will erect a new pillar to mark another unique aspect of Alberta's modern identity. It is a badge of local pride that distinguishes this vast province from everywhere else in North America – and almost anywhere else in the world. For more than 70 years, successive provincial governments have been proud to declare that Alberta is not home to a single black or Norway rat.

A triumphant mobilisation against rats has seen them expunged from every corner of the province. Supposedly there are no rats in its capital city, Edmonton, despite a population of nearly a million people. The municipal sewers and grain stores are free from the rustle of rodent feet. Most people here have never seen a rat. Even the hard-bitten Albertan dairy farmers will openly admit they are terrified of a creature the province has declared as its mortal enemy and somehow been able to keep at bay.

I have travelled here from Vancouver, where my brother and his family live and where rats are as common as in any populous city, to witness this remarkable success story for myself. For Alberta boasts the triumphant realisation of a distant dream to which humanity has aspired for centuries: life without rats.

Walking through Lloydminster by day in the North American sunshine, everything is displayed in bright primary colours. The sky is presidential blue and crisp shadows cut across the sidewalks like border markers of their own. But at dusk in these edgelands, the light muddies. The traffic lights suspended on steel poles over six lanes of highway traffic on the main drag shimmer in the twilight. The hulking Husky oil refinery on the edge of town coruscates like a battle cruiser coasting the prairies.

I am heading to dinner on the recommendation of the clerk at the front desk of the motel where I am staying. She had told me about a grill house she described as 'only a couple of minutes away', though soon after setting off I realise she imagined I was driving, because everyone drives everywhere here. Instead I walk along the side of the highway, tasting petrol and gravel kicked up by the supersized tyres of the procession of SUVs that speed past, blackening the snow pushed to the side of the road with grit and exhaust.

It is Sunday evening and the bars are busy with families watching the local ice hockey team, the Edmonton Oilers, on walls bedecked with plasma screens. Out back the bins are overflowing with half-eaten burgers and other delectable rodent offerings. I stare into the darkness with the headlights of passing cars casting my shadow on the wall and wonder: can there really be no rats?

In the distance, over the roar of passing cars, I hear the long blast of a freight train of the Canadian Pacific Railway passing through. I had explored the railway sidings earlier in the day and marvelled at the fireman-red locomotive engines and the rusty parade they towed behind them at a pace slow enough to run alongside. It is back along these railway tracks where the roots of this story lie. For the history of modern Alberta cannot be told without the history of the

Canadian Pacific Railway, which was built across the province in the 1880s as part of the rail line stretching thousands of miles east to west. The train hauled out cattle, horses, wheat and dairy products and hauled in settlers to exploit the new, untapped riches. And with them came rats.

There are three rat species native to Canada: muskrats, large, semi-aquatic species that live in wetlands; pack rats (also called bushy-tailed wood rats), like dormice in the UK distinguishable by their fluffy tails, and the magnificent but sadly dwindling Ord's kangaroo rat. Possessing ginger fur and large hind-legs that can propel it away from foes in 2-metre long hops, the Ord's rat is now one of the most threatened species in Alberta. It has suffered as its preferred habitat of sparsely vegetated prairie land has been carved up with roads, farmland and oil and gas developments, meaning isolated pockets of populations can no longer interconnect. Without this strength in numbers, they are vanishing one by one.

Brown rats were unheard of in Alberta until the railway was up and running. Soon these strange creatures were turning up across the province. The first record of any such rat in Alberta was in 1913, when five were spotted in a railway yard in the city of Lethbridge (about 120 miles south of Calgary). Then, in 1921, a captured specimen from elsewhere in the province was sent to the University of Alberta's zoology department, newly formed by a biologist called William Rowan. Many years later, in 1952, Mr Rowan recounted in a letter receiving that first rat and his fears over the subsequent invasion that occurred.

'Since then numerous instances of rats at railway yards have been reported,' he wrote. 'We have undoubtedly been getting a double dosage for a matter of many years, from both west and east. The only effective remedy, to my mind, lies with control on the railways.'

By that stage rats had already expanded along the growing railway network. In 1944, a 'rat survey' had been distributed among agents of the Northern Alberta Railway Company to determine the scale of the problem. Wanted posters were also placed in station waiting-rooms, asking the public to report any suspected rodents to the authorities, or take the law into their own hands.

A railway agent at the northern hamlet of Kinuso reported a small rat discovered within a 3-tonne shipment of coal, having built its nest in a tiny air pocket. A report of the discovery by the railway superintendent J. E. Deakin explained: 'The rat was immediately killed. The agent states that there is no doubt in his mind that it was a rat as he has seen similar rats in Britain.'

Another rat was discovered and killed in a box car in the nearby hamlet of Thorhild, while an agent at Eaglesham reported two brown rats frozen to death in a box car operated by the Canadian Pacific Railway Company and used for grain loading. In his summary to the provincial authorities of the number of incidents he had discovered, Mr Deakin admitted that the state of Alberta was now facing up to a serious invasion. 'The information available indicates it will take the combined efforts of all to prevent these animals getting a foothold in the province and becoming an exceptionally destructive pest,' he wrote in a letter to the local health department in November 1945.

More troubling still was the discovery that alongside these pioneer railway rats, larger colonies were starting to become established across farmland along Alberta's eastern border with Saskatchewan. The first of these Saskatchewan colonies was recorded in the 1920s, with the rats then extending their range north-west by an estimated 15 miles every year. By tooth, claw and determined fecundity, this was the inexorable progress of rat trench warfare.

By 1950, it was decided something had to be done. Responsibility for rat control was shifted from the government of Alberta's Department of Health to its Department of Agriculture and rats were officially included under the 1942 Agricultural Pests Act, meaning every person, landowner and municipality had an obligation to destroy any rat they encountered. A separate amendment to the act agreed in 1950 placed a stipulation on every municipality in Alberta to appoint a pest-control inspector to coordinate reduction efforts. Alberta's war on the rat was born.

Writing a letter to his superior in September 1950, the deputy minister of agriculture, Oliver Stanley Longman, outlined the details of the new Rat Control Programme. It included:

Acquiring pickled rat specimens to use as visual aids in public meetings and at schools.

Acquiring and caging live rats for similar purposes. It is recommended that district agriculturalists serving areas immediately threatened should address the pupils in every school room to familiarise themselves with the nature of the rodent, means of control, and what notion they should take if they should see any of the rodents in their communities … also give instruction to local farmers, municipal officials, railway and other transport employees on the identification and eradification [sic] of rats when found.

All district agriculturalists should be approved by the Department of Health as official fumigators for the use of cyanide gas.

Each municipality be required to appoint an official whose duty shall be to familiarise himself with methods of rat control.

Official notices be prepared and printed which will designate any premises on which rats are found.

The department render financial assistance to municipal districts, cities, towns.

The province of Alberta is blessed with a geography its governors believed placed it in a unique position from which to coordinate this battle and successfully repel the rats colonising everywhere else in North America. Blocked by the Rocky Mountains on its western border with British Columbia, the Arctic tundra of the Northwest Territories to the north and the empty open plains of Montana to the south, it is only along Alberta's eastern border where there is a sufficient concentration of people and agriculture for colonies of rats to expand in any great number.

It was here in the 1950s that it was decided to focus the bulk of their defending forces, and in particular a 600km-long and 29km-wide section of borderland running from Cold Lake in the north to the Montana border in the south through seven different municipalities. This eastern front was designated the Rat Control Zone, and remains in force today.

The immediate priority at a time when few had ever encountered a rat was ensuring the local populace knew their enemy. Rat-control conferences were held in towns in eastern Alberta and thousands of pamphlets and posters distributed advising people on how best to eliminate rats. Various highly toxic substances, including arsenic and strychnine, were advocated alongside the then relatively new anticoagulant, warfarin.

First marketed as a rodenticide in 1948, the substance that would go on to become the world's most commonly used method of rat disposal was still in its experimental stages by the time it was deployed in Alberta. Unlike other rodenticides, warfarin killed rats by causing them to haemorrhage slowly over time, meaning they did not learn to avoid the poisoned bait until it was too late.

One health newsletter from 1951 headlined 'Prince Albert region staff makes war upon rats' described the lethal impact of warfarin on rodents living in the city dump on the north side of the North Saskatchewan River, which according to the article 'offered an excellent testing place for a concerted well-planned kill'.

Its author marvels: 'The dump was literally teeming with rats. Bait mixed by machine included warfarin, freshly ground cornmeal and mineral oil. The rats liked it and a great advantage was that the wily rodents did not become bait shy. Rats by the thousands ate the bait and for many two feedings were enough to end their prowls. Pictures of dead and dying rodents among the litter of the dump looked impressive but gave only a hint of the destruction as many died in hiding places.'

This was a new chemical age, one where humans possessed an unshakeable belief in the power of these new synthetic potions to tame and reorder the natural world around them. Poisons were modern and exciting hallmarks of progress and many locals took to the mission with unnerving zeal.

One letter in the Alberta provincial archives particularly recommended spraying DDT (the lethal chemical banned in subsequent decades after Rachel Carson exposed its horrifying impact on birds) over landfill to deter 'filthy, parasite-ridden and savage' rats. The unnamed author adds: 'This is actually a job for everybody. The entire formula for rat control can be summed up in 'build 'em out, starve 'em out, kill 'em'. Elsewhere, some in government mused upon dispatching teams of weasels along the border to help dispose of the rats – a suggestion William Rowan at the University of Alberta's zoology department promptly shot down as 'entirely inadequate to meet the rat threat'.

Despite this onslaught, by 1951, a year into the declaration of war, it seemed that everything the people of Alberta could throw at their new enemies was having little effect. That autumn, 30 rat infestations were confirmed along the eastern front. The following year, rats had occupied nearly half the length of the entire border. As an article in the *Edmonton Journal*, written in September 1952, described it: 'The invasion of rats exceeds belief.' A provincial government spokesman bluntly outlined the situation to the journalist: 'Rats are either invading eastern Alberta faster than the experts had predicted or extend over a greater invasion area than had been previously reported.'

It was time, the authorities concluded, to escalate the border skirmishes into an all-out assault. To lead it they recruited a hotelier from the Canadian city of Winnipeg who had newly established his own pest-control business. He also happened to possess a fitting name for a commander-in-chief of the campaign: Napoleon Poulin.

The way Napoleon Louis Poulin told it, he was born to kill rats. In an interview with the *Winnipeg Tribune* in 1962, five years before his death at the age of 73, he reflected on a lifelong loathing of rodents. He was born on a farm south of the Winnipeg town of St Malo in 1894 and as a youngster begged his parents for a dog. They steadfastly refused, but then in 1902 Napoleon found a stray puppy on their land and secretly kept it as a pet. He housed the beloved dog in a grain shed in secret from his parents, and would sneak out of bed each morning to feed and play with it. One morning he walked over to the grain store and discovered to his horror the puppy being eaten by rats. 'I had a little puppy dog and the rats chewed him to bits,' he explained to the reporter. 'Ever since then I've been killing them back.'

Before he arrived in Alberta, Napoleon Poulin was only just starting out in what he discovered as his true calling. Previously, he had worked for 30-odd years in the hospitality trade, expanding something of an empire in hotels and boarding houses. His particular business model was buying cut-price hotels in run-down parts of town that had been condemned by health inspectors. He would then personally go in to rid the buildings of whatever pests they were infested with before reopening them at a tidy profit.

He had flipped half a dozen or so hotels in this manner when the inspector who presented him with a new health certificate suggested he might be in the wrong business. Napoleon agreed and in 1946, Poulin's Pest Control was born.

With his business steadily growing, the Alberta government's decision to put the contract of exterminating the rats on its eastern border out to tender proved a once-in-a-lifetime opportunity. A natural-born entrepreneur, Napoleon Poulin drew up a list of terms too good for the government to refuse.

A letter in the provincial archives dated 13 February 1952 outlines his proposal. Poulin provided assurances he would 'personally supervise the control programme', while his trusted foreman from Winnipeg would preside over all 'eradication methods, poisons and other materials used'. His estimated costs for the wages and living expenses for his foreman spending six weeks in the field would be $450 (about 4,500 Canadian dollars today) and his own travelling expenses would amount to $150. He also requested $300 of 'materials consisting of arsenic, warfarin etc'.

Seeing the public relations potential of undertaking and securing victory in such an ambitious war against the rat, Napoleon also offered his would-be employers a sweetener: 'Mr Poulin is willing to undertake the programme as an experiment and at the same time to establish his ability of eradicating rats with a view to obtaining more profitable contracts at a later time.'

The deal was done, but even in spite of Poulin waiving his fee, $150,000 (about $1.5 million today) of public money was still spent on exterminating rats over the following two years. Poulin and his pest controllers (a hand-picked team of six of his best workers) embarked on an all-out rampage. Between June 1952 and July 1953, nearly 64,000kg of arsenic trioxide tracking powder was used to treat 8,000 buildings over an area 20 to 50km wide and 300km long. So much of the tracking powder (which traces rodent movements as well as poisoning them) was laid down that secondary poisoning of livestock, poultry and pets occurred for up to five years after the treatment.

Their victims were logged in painstaking detail in local ledgers. In the town of Provost: 'In baled straw 80 rats killed June 54. 40 later.' In Acadia Valley: 'Water soluble warfarin used with good consumption and results.' And on March 1954 in Lloydminster: '122 rats killed by monoxide ... arsenic granary burrows, 21 killed.'

One photograph of Poulin and his crew shows them standing triumphantly beside a mountain of dead rats. Driving the invaders back to within 10km of the eastern border finally put the Albertan authorities on the front foot. The Department of Agriculture set about establishing the policing of the rat-control zone in perpetuity. Napoleon

Poulin's name, meanwhile, was secured in pest-control history. In 1955, a triumphant *Winnipeg Free Press* article described him as 'the man who killed 10 million rats'.

That morning I am driving out of town to the nearby County of Vermillion River, a small agricultural community of about 3,700 residents, to join the first rat border patrol of the year. Over winter in Alberta, temperatures commonly range between minus 5 and minus 15°C, and for weeks will stand at minus 35°C, with the fields covered in heavy drifts of snow. Driving along the main highway, the few trees I see lining the roadside are scorched and still, petrified by this brutal deep freeze.

Only specialist creatures can typically withstand such temperatures, but rats use their cunning to survive in a state of torpor. Unable to hibernate, they instead locate a food source and dig a nest as deep and warm as possible next to it where they wait it out until spring. Previous years of patrols have occasionally discovered rats burrowed into grain stores or hay bales to see out the winter before emerging when the snow melts.

This happens in Alberta around late March. It takes many weeks for the layers of snow and ice to dissolve into aquamarine puddles, revealing the yellowed prairie grass beneath. That is when all life starts to return to these open plains. As I drive, skeins of Canada geese arrow through the skies overhead, navigating their way northwards from their winter grounds in Mexico. And that too is when the rat inspectors head out on patrol, as hostilities resume for another year.

I meet Darin Beckett and his colleague Hannah Musterer at an industrial park of single-storey buildings prefabricated out of corrugated steel. Their office is situated next to a waste-disposal facility and a shop selling agricultural chemicals. Darin greets me from behind a desk bearing a framed photograph of him in a high-vis vest and brandishing a shotgun, holding a dead rat by the tail. That is the first and only rat he has ever shot, he tells me, while helping out the previous year with an infestation at the town of Provost a hundred miles south along the border. 'My first trophy,' he grins.

A moustachioed man in his late fifties wearing an Alberta Rat Patrol cap and hoodie, Darin has been employed by the county for the past 10 years. Previously he worked for 22 years as a middle manager at an agricultural supply company before applying to join the rat patrol. Unlike his predecessor Napoleon Poulin, he claims no origin story for why he decided to join the frontline in Alberta's war on rats, only that he needed a 'change of pace'. But he is deadly serious about the importance of his job. 'We can't allow them to get established,' he tells me. 'It took a lot of work to clean them out. We need to make sure we don't regress, go backwards and have infestations again.'

There are two key periods of the year for the rat inspectors: in early April and again in October. During this time Darin and Hannah head out in their truck touring farmyards, fields and any other human habitation for the first six miles from the border into Alberta. Overall, they carry out in the region of 700 checks a year (a process that is replicated by their fellow inspectors in every municipal county along the border). In 10 years, he says, there have been two positive rat IDs – the first in a recycling processing plant in Lloydminster, where rats managed to sneak inside, hiding in a batch of cardboard sent from Saskatchewan. Darin and his fellow inspectors laced the entire facility with bait and killed three rats.

Then there was the aforementioned outbreak in Provost. Overall in Alberta last year, he says, there was in the region of 300 reported sightings with people contacting a specialist rat hotline – although only 31 were confirmed as brown rats. In spring, muskrats moving between water bodies are the most commonly misidentified species.

'Doing our checks I'm sometimes disappointed we don't find them more often but on the other hand I think, hey, this programme started in the fifties is still working,' Darin says. 'What I am doing means something and it helps out the farmers.'

Darin is a farmer himself, he tells me, as we head out in his truck: a jet black RAM 2500 with *Alberta Rat Control* lacquered on the side. He and Hannah sit in the front while I take the back seat as we rattle down the back-country roads. In the footwell next to me are moulded blocks of blue bait laced with rodenticide.

Darin's family were originally from England and came to Alberta in the early twentieth-century wave of immigration. His farm is 40km away from the office at Vermillion River and has been in the family for about 80 years. Darin operates it as a hobby rather than a commercial enterprise, but still grows crops across 400 acres and owns 60 pairs of cow and calves. His children, though, are moving to the provincial capital in Edmonton. He tells me young people are not interested in the quiet rural life, preferring to move to the big cities. Farmers are dying off and there is nobody to replace them, and as a result the farms themselves are becoming abandoned.

Roughly the size of Texas and with a population of around 4.3 million, if Alberta were a country it would be the fifth-largest oil-producing nation on earth. The vast majority – around 160 billion barrels of recoverable oil – comes from the Alberta tar sands. The magical properties of these sands were first discovered by First Nations communities, who boiled them to extract the bitumen to waterproof their canoes. In the early twentieth century, experimental research work started on the oil sands, initially focusing on extracting the bitumen as a means of paving roads. The first large-scale oil-sands mine was established in the mid twentieth century – around the same time as Alberta started killing its rats – laying the foundations for what has since become one of the most environmentally destructive oil operations on earth.

The tar sands are either mined from below, blasting huge amounts of water and steam to bring it to the surface, or, where the bitumen layer is shallow enough, in open pits. Since the turn of the twenty-first century, an estimated 2 million acres of boreal forest has been felled or burned by wildfire in the tar sands region – causing scars on the landscape so huge they are visible from space. A heady smell of burning tyres hangs over the sands, while Indigenous lands around many of the operations have been devastated.

The tar sands region is in the far north and north-east of Alberta, well away from where we are driving. Oil production along the Saskatchewan border is of the more conventional kind. We drive past fragments of old woodland amid the pastures, copses of willow, poplar and birch. Many of the farmer's fields are studded with black oil silos and the pumpjacks known as nodding donkeys. Darin says a farmer can make anything between 2,000 and 5,000 dollars a month letting the large producers pump oil on their land – so pretty much everyone does.

Hannah, who is 24 and born and bred in the area, graduated from college in Vermillion in 2019 and took on a summer job with the local Department of Agriculture and Environment, working on vegetation management. When a job opened up on the rat patrols she immediately applied. When we meet she is two and a half years into the role and still waiting to kill her first rat. 'My friends are all jealous,' she says of the job. 'Particularly about our Rat Patrol uniform and hats. Everyone wants a hat, but only pest-control officers can wear these.'

We tour the various farms Darin and Hannah have earmarked on their schedule, searching hay bales, grain stores and barns for any sign of gnaw-marks or other rat disturbance. One farm in particular has been concerning Darin because the land is littered with bits of old machinery and poorly maintained outbuildings – but the owners are not around to let us in for a closer look. Instead we peer in from the outside at the rusting hulks of tractors. As well as searching for rats, their job is also about ensuring potential habitat for the rodents is removed. In recent years the old timber hip-roof barns built by the original settlers have started to be replaced by modern constructions, much to the sadness of some traditionalists. Grain is now increasingly stored in steel ventilated hoppers raised off the ground so rats and other critters cannot get inside. Growing up here, Darin says, he knew old farmers who told stories about barns being so infested by rats they killed them by hitting them with a tennis racket. But these tall tales have been lost with a whole generation. Now the environment here has been sanitised; de-ratted.

On one of the new-style farms, with gleaming elevated steel drums of grain and not a single haystack out of place, we stop and chat to a farm-owner, Scott, aged in his fifties. The farm started with his grandfather around a century ago and has been in the family ever since. He took over in 1996.

He has only seen a rat once. He was about 10 years old and saw it scuttling under a bin full of cattle feed. The family dog, a border collie named Rusty, quickly bolted out and

killed it. That one encounter was enough, Scott says, to
sustain a lifelong terror. He admits that given their almost
total absence from the landscape it is something of an
irrational fear – akin to being worried about a shark attack
in the English Channel. But as he acknowledges, it is a fear
borne out of ignorance, knowing the rat through myth
rather than reality. 'I would be very worried if there are rats
here,' he says. 'I've never really experienced what rats can do.'

Around a decade ago, Lianne McTavish, a professor in the
history of art, design and visual culture at the University of
Alberta, co-authored a paper examining how the provincial
government had sought to educate its citizens about rats.
The researchers compared the imagery used in different rat
posters from the 1950s onwards, created as part of the public-
information drive alongside the killings. Commissioned by
the government and distributed among thousands of schools,
public buildings, farms and events such as rodeos, these
posters were intended to mobilise the civil populace and
keep their enemy in the forefront of their minds. As outlined
by the then deputy minister of agriculture, Oliver Stanley, in
1950: 'The Alberta government isn't taking any chances that
the people of Alberta won't know a Norway rat when they
see one.' He stressed the need to make his innocent public
what he termed 'rat conscious'.

In part this was done through putting dead rat specimens
on display. As McTavish explains in her paper, initially 25
dead rats were sent by Napoleon Poulin, which he had
recently killed in Winnipeg. These specimens were then
entombed in plastic by local pest officers and dispatched
around the province. The dead rats proved something of a

hit. In 1954, 50 additional corpses were distributed and in 1961 a further 70 sent out.

As McTavish writes, against the backdrop of the cull, the posters, which were also distributed by the authorities, leant heavily on the language and imagery of conflict. One early poster headlined 'The rats are coming' shows Alberta as a lone white space on a map of North America surrounded by an army of menacing-looking rodents. 'Let's keep 'em out!' is written three times on the page. Another poster shows a rat strung up by the tail. 'The only good rat, is a dead rat,' it reads.

At the time, any member of the public reporting an outbreak or contacting the authorities for additional information would have received a fold-out flyer entitled 'Kill Rats with Warfarin or Pival'. The latter anticoagulant was first synthesised during the Second World War and further developed by the US government.

While ostensibly the posters were designed to educate the citizens of Alberta about the presence of rats and help distinguish them from native muskrats, pack rats and pocket gophers, as far as possible the designers also demonised their subject. One poster looks like that of a low-budget horror film, portraying a close-up rat, fangs bared and claws razor-sharp, with the outline of Alberta in red reflected in its jet-black eyes. Particular attention is paid to the tail – the part of the rat anatomy that inspires the most human disgust. It is inevitably depicted curled across the page, whip-like behind the advancing rodents.

The 1950s was the 'dream decade' of advertising, with post-war economies rebounding and people eager to spend their increasingly disposable income after years of paucity. As with many adverts of the era, be it Coca Cola, diamonds, tobacco or cars, the emphasis of the rat posters was on the family. In these images the idealised Alberta farming family was white, patriarchal, homogenous and, crucially, rodent-free. McTavish cites one 1954 pamphlet depicting a farmer in baggy overalls and smoking a pipe, proudly standing alongside his wife, wearing high heels and a fashionable dress, and his son. 'There are no rats on our farmstead,' he proclaims. 'Because we keep it clean!' In all of the many posters and pamphlets circulated by the Alberta government during the 1950s, McTavish says, that is the only one that shows a woman.

Seventy years on and they are still killing any rat that dares step foot in Alberta, but nowadays it is a woman in overall charge of the programme. I meet Karen Wickerson, Alberta Agriculture's rat and pest programme specialist, at her headquarters in Airdrie, a few hours south of Edmonton. An exhibition celebrating 70 years of the rat programme has been set up inside the entrance hall of the building, including old Victor rat traps and some of the original public information posters I recognise from my research. One catches my eye, a nightmarish version of a rat, claws splayed, with the headline: 'Rat on a Rat.'

'It obviously worked very well and contributed in a large part to the success of the programme,' Karen tells me, sitting in her office. 'I don't try and put fear into people like that about rats but just try and educate them about why we don't want them to establish.'

Karen is also an outsider here. Originally from Ontario, she arrived in Alberta 23 years ago after travelling east to do a ski season in the Rocky Mountains, and stayed. Unlike many in the province she had first-hand experience of rats. Long before she started working for Alberta Agriculture, she was employed by a veterinary practice that was hired by a company conducting medical experiments on rats. Her job, as an animal health technologist, was to care for the rats housed at the clinic. 'They are smart,' she says. 'There's a reason why they are the most invasive species in the world. I respect them because they can adapt to pretty much any environment, and thrive.'

For the past decade or so Karen has worked for Alberta's Department of Agriculture, and after the longstanding head of the rat programme retired, she was hired as a replacement. She admits the job comes with a huge amount of responsibility. 'Mainly I want to keep Alberta rat free and continue the success of the programme,' she says. Her terror is being the person who finally lets them in.

I wonder if she ever has any rat anxiety dreams. It is something I have experienced on occasion over the course of writing this book, when the rodents scuttle into the subconscious and gnaw on the edges of your thoughts. 'I had a rat dream last night,' she says, laughing, before a serious look spreads across her face. 'I really feel the importance of its success.'

She defines the province's rat-free status as meaning that while occasionally rodents do emerge they are dealt with promptly to ensure none ever breed. The previous year, she says, officers dealt with 35 reported rats around Alberta and two infestations on the eastern border. The rodent sightings are reported via a dedicated hotline launched in 2015 – 310-Rats – and an email address, which she established after taking on the role.

One regular route that lone rats run is over the Rocky Mountains, where they hitch a ride into Alberta inside trucks or even the engines of family cars that have stopped en route for a picnic lunch. The animals rarely make it though, and even the ones that survive the perilous drive over twisting mountain roads will not be able to establish a food source in time once they have made it into Alberta.

There are also occasional reports of rats being kept as pets – something that is prohibited. Karen tells me about a recent example in Calgary where, following a bad break-up, a man phoned the authorities to tell them his ex-girlfriend had two pet rats at home. Karen arranged a visit and the pets were confiscated and transferred to a pet rescue centre in the neighbouring province of British Columbia. She admits it was a wrench taking the rats (fancy rats like my own pets Molly and Ermintrude) away from their heartbroken owner, who was only in her early twenties. 'As an animal lover I understand … but we've come so far, I wouldn't want to do anything to damage the integrity of the programme or put it at risk,' she says.

Alberta's unique international status means Karen is often contacted by people from across the world. Recently she had a woman phone her out of the blue from an island on the Caribbean. 'She told me she had a rat in her yard.' Karen smiles. 'I told her to put a trap out.'

After leaving Karen, I arrange a trip to the provincial archives in Edmonton to read up on the history of the programme and see some more of the posters for myself. In the gift shop I buy a replica of a 1950s poster. It portrays a greasy, black-furred specimen surrounded by the messaging: 'He's a menace to health, home and industry. Kill him!' When I eventually make it back home I get the poster framed and hang it on the wall above the cage where my two pet rats happily live, oblivious (I hope) to the unique fear and loathing humans reserve for their species.

Edmonton is a city of tunnels, even if there are no rats lurking among them. The deep winters here mean its citizens have long sought alternative routes underground. One such tunnel was constructed between 1927 and 1928 on the eve of the Great Depression to link traffic downtown with a newly planned northern extension to the city. Opened by the mayor on 12 October 1928, who praised the tunnel as a triumph of modern engineering, locals referred to it instead as the Rathole. Prone to flash flooding and trailers getting blocked, the Rathole was finally closed for good in 2000. Now only a small plaque and a pile of commemorative concrete blocks mark its spot, and Edmonton's inhabitants scurry elsewhere.

Underneath downtown runs a series of pedestrian tunnels known as the Pedway. Originally approved by city planners in 1968 as a traffic-free route that could transport people in comfort and safety away from the gruelling winters above ground, over subsequent decades the Pedway has morphed into a 13km labyrinth connecting 40 buildings, including city hall, the law courts, theatres and hotels. It is as close to a human equivalent of a rat burrow as you are likely to experience.

During my stopover in the city I could not pass up the opportunity to see the tunnels for myself. The motel concierge, though, seemed surprised that I wanted to walk there. Just be careful, he cautioned, as he pointed out the directions. It soon became clear, walking through the scrubby local park next to the motel on the way to downtown, what he was talking about. Syringes littered the floor while an air of unspoken menace hung over the park. I walked past a man openly injecting himself in the groin by the side of a busy six-lane highway. Others huddled in shady groups around bus stops, their backs turned to the traffic.

It was around 6 p.m. on a Tuesday night and the time when city centre offices should be emptying out, but the streets around downtown were oddly quiet. As I located a Pedway entrance at the Edmonton city centre mall, a crowd jostled at the door. Inside, the mall was nearly deserted and most of the shops shuttered up as I made it down to the basement level.

I hadn't quite anticipated what the Pedway might look like, but it made a shocking sight. The tunnels were largely empty save for scattered groups of the presumably homeless and destitute. Some sat alone with their heads between their legs, other sprawled glassy-eyed on the floor or wandered about with the stiff-limbed marionette movements common to addicts. Two girls in their late teens, or at most early twenties, were hunched together with their backs against the subway wall, surrounded by discarded orange peel (the fruit is known to help alleviate some of the pain of heroin withdrawal).

A few after-work commuters hurried past on their way to one of the rail stations that the Pedway connects to. I kept walking, too. But each passageway revealed a similar scene. Here was a literal underclass, trapped in their tunnels as the city carried on above.

A few days before I visited, the local paper, *The Edmonton Journal*, started running a three-part series into the city's drug crisis. Between January and October 2021, 1,372 Albertans had died of drug poisoning, making it the deadliest year on record. To investigate the causes, a reporter travelled across Edmonton reporting on the areas most blighted by drugs – including the Pedway, where she joined a group of volunteers who spend their evenings walking the tunnels distributing clean syringes, pipes and tin foil as well as chocolate bars to help reduce the impact of drug poisoning. Overdoses are common here, and teams of emergency first-responders are regularly scrambled underground.

The drugs most commonly used are fentanyl and methamphetamine. The former, in particular, has exploded across North America in recent years in the fallout from the opioid crisis, which led to mass overprescribing of the highly addictive drugs given as painkillers. A recent study of the wastewater of Canadian cities found Edmonton to have the second highest level of fentanyl in its wastewater after Vancouver and the highest level of methamphetamine. Fentanyl is locally nicknamed Down, and the effect is similar to that seen in people smoking Spice on the streets of the UK. The drug leaves them frozen like statues to the spot.

Were these pedestrian tunnels anywhere else in the western world, then rats would most likely be here too, feasting on the discarded fruit peelings and candy bars. So often are rats associated with scenes of such urban dystopia that on some level they are regarded as a cause, rather than a symptom. Yet in the Pedway, just as elsewhere in Alberta, the rodents are of course absent.

After I had emerged from underground, I thought about all the things I had encountered among Alberta's sprawling oilfields, gargantuan highways and the addicts of the Edmonton Pedway that rats are commonly blamed for: environmental destruction, greed, litter, disease and municipal decay. When we seek to demonise others, it is so often to mask our own failings, for these are problems that, like rats themselves, follow humanity wherever it has spread. You can wipe out every rat in a city, seal up the rat holes and lock down the borders, but the problems of our own species remain.

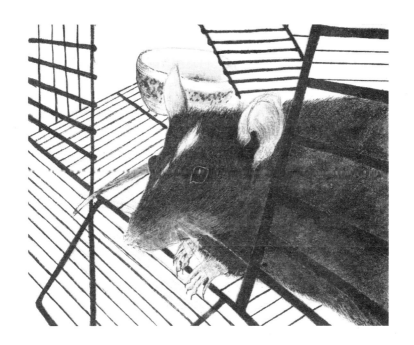

CHAPTER NINE

Fancy

In his book, *The Thing With Feathers*, US ornithologist Noah Strycker devotes a section to the brief and supercharged lifecycle of the hummingbird. The world's smallest warm-blooded vertebrates, hummingbirds have evolved a rocket-boosted metabolic rate in order to produce enough energy to survive. Their hearts have been measured at more than 1,200 beats per minute (roughly 6 times faster than the maximum speed of a human) while their lungs can process more than 250 breaths per minute to pump sufficient oxygen into their muscles. Hummingbirds, Strycker writes, 'live at the edge of physical possibility'.

Rats lead similarly strenuous existences. As with hummingbirds and a host of other smaller organisms, rats are furry furnaces that must continually generate enough heat to regulate their bodies. Every single minute, their hearts beat between 330 and 480 times and they take around 85 breaths. By means of comparison, a typical human resting heart beats around 60 to 100 times a minute and our respiratory rate is between 12 and 16 breaths.

As Stryker notes, various studies have pointed out that mammals expend roughly one billion heartbeats over the course of their entire existence. For long-lived mammals such as humans and whales, this countdown spans out with luck over many decades on earth. Rats get around two years. Possibly three, if they are lucky. A single month of their existence has been calculated as comparable to approximately three human years.

Holding Molly one evening in my lap as she devoured a chip of dried banana, her little heart pumping against my thigh, I wondered how many beats she had left. She was by now just over two years old and beginning to show her age. Normally so immaculately groomed, her soft grey fur was increasingly unkempt. Her tail drooped behind her like a loose shoelace.

She had also started to develop hind-leg degeneration, a typical condition among geriatric rats when their back legs begin to drag as they walk. This impacts on the normally balletic balance of the rat. While Molly remained as willing as ever, she could no longer trust her body as she once could. Whenever she clambered up the outside bars of the cage or scampered along a tabletop, we stayed watchfully close by to ensure she didn't fall.

Ermintrude was also visibly ageing. A few months previously she had developed a small lump on her chest. Female rats are prone to fibroadenomas (benign tumours in their mammary glands), which are also common in humans. The lump was giving her no obvious discomfort and she was as energetic and affectionate as before, still able to groom herself and with her voracious appetite undiminished. We were far more worried about the impact on her of being left alone without the sister she had lived alongside her entire life. Having witnessed the deep social structures and extended families of rats living in the wild, it felt cruel to leave such a gregarious creature pining alone.

We needed expert advice beyond the rat forums of the internet. I had previously been in touch with the National Fancy Rat Society about attending one of their shows. According to their events page, one was coming up at a community hall in Scawsby, Doncaster, not far from where we lived. While we supposed our two ageing rats would not pass muster under the scrupulous gaze of the show judges, we thought it would be a good place to meet some breeders and to canvas opinion about how best to care for Molly and Ermintrude in their dotage.

The National Fancy Rat Society was formed on 13 January 1976, following a chance meeting at a bus stop. The two founding members, Geoff Izzard, a herpetologist who bred rats to feed to his snakes, and Joan Pearce, a teacher, had met while waiting to go home outside the London Championship Show in 1974. The pair had left disappointed. The show, which still runs today, is one of the country's largest exhibitions of small animals, but back then rats were a rarity. Indeed, Joan had attended with the express hope of meeting some rats but couldn't find a single one among the mass of gerbils, hamsters and rabbits.

While waiting for the bus home, the pair started chatting and quickly discovered a mutual interest in rats. They stayed in touch and two years later decided to form their own

club – the National Fancy Rat Society (NFRS). At first, they
held displays alongside other small mammals but on 15 April
1978, the first ever show dedicated solely to rats took place at
an address on Grove Road in Surbiton, on the southern
fringes of London. Reading this history, carefully researched
by the club's current president, Ann Storey, I wonder what
the denizens of the archetype of affluent suburbia would
have made of a rat show being held on their doorstep.

Today the NFRS is the Crufts of the rodent world,
celebrating the cream of Britain's rats. The society hosts
shows across the country at which a judging panel awards
rosettes for the health, vigour and beauty of various breeds
based upon strict criteria. There are dozens of small regional
shows held throughout the year and five championship
events where cups, and even rat-shaped trophies, are awarded
to the most impressive entries. The results are meticulously
recorded in the society's bi-monthly magazine, *Pro-Rat-a*.

The Scawsby show is one of the less high profile in the
NFRS calendar, but when we arrive the community hall is
nonetheless busy with people, and rats. The entrants are
lounging around in plastic boxes on a generous bed of
sawdust with scraps of cucumber to nibble (and keep them
hydrated). The judges occupy a seat at the head table,
studiously inspecting the rats before them. The breeders
loiter nearby, but at a respectful distance. I later discover it is
strictly prohibited for any entrants to identify which rat
belongs to them in order to ensure objectivity in the judging.

Stalls selling rat-themed clothes, jewellery and soft
furnishings to adorn cages are dotted about the room. We buy
a new bed for our rats with a pocket stitched into it to enable
them to hunker down together inside. The world of the fancy,
as enthusiasts call it, is evidently a small one, with almost all of
the 50 or so people inside the room appearing to know one

another. An excitable buzz hangs over the tables, as well as an element of horse-trading as rats are passed around.

We sit and start talking to one breeder, Julie Oliver, who has just been presented with two rats promised to her a while back by a friend. They are rex rats, known for their ruffled fur and curly whiskers. Julie hands one to Liz, who eagerly strokes it in her lap. The other clambers over Julie's shoulders as we talk.

A primary school teacher, Julie is a veteran of the rat show scene. She has been breeding since 1998 and at any one time estimates she has an adult population of around 50 rats living in a converted garage in her Cambridgeshire home. She has previously displayed a couple of gold championship rats and says she has several plastic boxes at home filled with rosettes from previous shows.

If this sounds like bragging, then it most certainly is not. As a journalist I have written about Crufts and interviewed various participants in the ultra-competitive world of dog shows. Rat shows, Julie explains, are very different. Breeders are genuinely delighted to see each other's entries and nobody is in it for the glory. As for money, she says, most people including herself struggle to break even. They do it instead purely for the love of rats.

'It tends to attract people that are perhaps a bit alternative,' Julie tells me. 'Probably a higher percentage of eccentric people shall we say. People that are perhaps neurodivergent, there a lot of those in the rat fancy.' I note, looking around the room, that nearly all the enthusiasts appear to be women. 'If you want to find men,' Julie says, 'go and look for the rabbit and mice breeders'.

On the eve of a show, Julie carefully clips the claws of the rats she is intending to enter. She shows me the scratches on her hands as proof of that morning's work. Some of the paler varieties also require having their tails cleaned using a toothbrush and washing-up liquid. Otherwise, the meticulous personal grooming of rats means she does not need to intervene with their already glossy fur. The condition of the fur, she explains, is really down to their diet. Julie feeds her rats four different types of breakfast cereal, seeds and a rabbit food base.

She acquired her first rat in her first week of university in Cardiff: a black and white hooded specimen called Oscar. He enjoyed more or less free rein of her student room, Julie recalls, shredding papers, stealing pens and hiding them under the bed along with the occasional slice of pizza. Sometimes she would smuggle him into lectures in her pocket or bag. She grins: 'Nobody really noticed and he didn't wander off too much.'

The owner of the pet shop in Cardiff market who sold Oscar to her advised, erroneously, that rats do better on their own. Over the years she has discovered the exact opposite. Rats don't just enjoy companionship, they depend on it, forging incredibly strong bonds and craving social contact.

She has noticed that as rats grow older and more frail, others within the colony will take on a caring responsibility, sleeping alongside them and ensuring they are still eating food. When one rat dies, she says, the others will often bury their cage mate under some bedding. She also thinks that rats grieve. Following a death, the group dynamic will inevitably shift, with new rats trying to assert themselves as leaders. She compares the complex hierarchical world of rats to that of chimpanzees.

There are no breeds in rat shows, just varieties. This is because the diverse array of pampered rodents luxuriating in their cages before me, their fur ranging from silver to a rich cinnamon to a deep steel blue, all belong to one single species – the common sewer rat.

The roots of this curious genesis lie in eighteenth-century Japan, where during the Edo period breeding rats to produce different coat colours was a popular pursuit. So popular, in fact, that several guidebooks on the subject were produced. The most famous texts are the *Yosotamanokakehashi*, published in 1775, and the *Chingansodategusa*, published in 1787. The former translates to 'A bridge to obtaining novel jewel-like nezumi'. While there is some uncertainty about whether 'nezumi' refers to a mouse or a rat, the Japanese researcher Takashi Kuramoto, who in 2011 published a history of the guidebook, says it almost certainly applies to the latter.

As the earliest known text on breeding rats, the book is a bible of the fancy. There are illustrated descriptions of various types, including the 'red-eyed white' (an ancestor of the modern-day lab rat) and the rare 'black-eyed white', prized as a portent of prosperity. Other varieties featured in the book are the 'bear rat' (black with a white crescent on its chest) and 'fox rat' (with a white belly and ruddy back). The book ends with a list of five pet shops that traded rats in what is today the city of Osaka, four of them located on a single street. Evidently the trade in rats was popular enough for money to be made.

The story of rat breeding in the west is a darker one, which speaks to our own troubled relationship with rodents. The first real evidence of it dates back to the rat pits of the mid nineteenth century, when such was the thirst for blood sport that a constant supply of rodents was required to be killed in front of the baying crowds.

Remember the landlord and notorious rat-pit proprietor of the Blue Anchor Tavern, Jimmy Shaw, mentioned in an earlier chapter? He is recorded as saying that at the height of its popularity he had 20 different families supplying him with rats from Clavering in Essex as well as a 'great quantity' from the north London borough of Enfield, which he described as 'a sort of headquarters for rat-ketchers [sic]'. On average, Shaw claimed, he shipped in between 300 and 700 rats a week.

Shaw also bred his own rats. Interviewed by the Victorian writer Henry Mayhew as part of his series on London's underclasses (which also included the royal rat-catcher Jack Black), Shaw demonstrated some of his tame rats, which he kept in cages in the sitting room. He showed Mayhew some piebald rats and a pink-eyed albino specimen. Mayhew recorded how Shaw handled the domestic rats 'without the least fear', which suggests it was highly unusual to meet anyone who kept them as pets.

The savagery of the rat pits was another reason why well-bred rodents were particularly sought after. Dogs would regularly suffer bites (and their handlers, too) as rats fought for their lives. It was presumed that country rats were far less disease-ridden than their urban counterparts, whose bites could lead to unpleasant infections, and domesticated ones were even better. Shaw himself confessed he had been bitten hundreds of times. 'If I had my will,' he told Mayhew, 'I wouldn't allow sewer ratting, for the rats in the shores eat up a great quantity of sewer filth and rubbish, and is another species of scavenger in their own way.'

Rat breeding soon led to a trade beyond the pits. Following the first scientific trial involving rats in 1828, from the mid nineteenth century they were increasingly used in laboratory experiments. A pet rat also became something of a sought-after accessory among the upper classes. The rat-catcher Jack Black, who operated his own breeding programme, boasted that he would sell them to 'well-bred young ladies in squirrel cages'.

Among those to own a pet rat was the author Beatrix Potter, who had an albino called Samuel. Potter, who was in her early forties at the time, adored her rat, to whom she dedicated her 1908 book, *The Tale of Samuel Whiskers*. She also produced a number of drawings: 'Studies of a tame rat "Sammy" from life.' One of the drawings, now held by the Victoria and Albert Museum, she entitled, 'The peculiar dream of Mr. Samuel Whiskers, upon the subject of Dutch cheese'.

I have often watched my own rats lost in inner thought and wondered what is flashing through their brains. Food, obviously, but they are also processing other, deeper reflections. In 2015, scientists at University College London measured brain activity in rats as they rested and found enhanced activity in their hippocampus cells. This is a part of the brain similar in both humans and rats, involved in spatial navigation and memory of places and events. The researchers suggested that this was the rats replaying memories of where they had been, forming mental maps and plotting their future activities. Thoughts which, very possibly, also included cheese.

Around the time Beatrix Potter took ownership of Samuel, the earliest rat shows were being held in Britain. According to Ann Storey's history of the NFRS, the first time fancy rats were actually displayed was on 24 October 1901, by a woman called Mary Douglas at the Aylesbury Fanciers' Show. There were apparently 15 different rats exhibited in one class and Mary won with a black and white hooded variety.

Storey describes Mary Douglas as the 'mother of the rat fancy'. She joined the National Mouse Club (which had formed in 1895) and lobbied to ensure that it would include two classes of rats in every show. By 1912, the society rebranded to become the National Mouse and Rat Club. In 1916, the London and Southern Counties Mouse and Rat Club was formed. It remains in existence today as the oldest area mouse and rat club in Britain.

Following the end of the First World War, however, the rat fancy fell out of favour. This coincided with the death of Mary Douglas in 1921, but the stories of horror from the trenches and declaration of national war on the rat must also have influenced enthusiasts. With the Rats and Mice (Destruction) Act passed in Parliament in 1919 and politicians and campaigners calling for the rat to be obliterated, it must have been difficult, if not considered heretical, to continue a society celebrating the beauty and gentle nature of such a demonised creature.

By 1934, the London and Southern Counties Mouse and Rat Club dropped the word 'Rat' from its title. In 1957, the National Mouse and Rat Club followed suit. In 1962, according to Storey, a Welsh fancier called R. G. Phillips attempted to form a National Rat Club but failed to ignite enough enthusiasm.

However, the 'fancy' was slowly building back. In 1968, the London and Southern Counties Mouse Club succumbed to demand and agreed to reintroduce classes for rats. That same year the club reinstated the word 'Rat' in its name, which it has kept to this day. Then a few years later, the NFRS was born.

Nowadays it is the largest of a number of rat clubs across the country. The North of England Rat Society runs its own show calendar and longevity awards. Rats who make it to 28 months are awarded bronze, 32 months for silver, 36 months for gold and 40 months for platinum. The long-lived rats are honoured in a hall-of-fame section on the society website, and receive honourable mention in its quarterly magazine, *Rattitude.*

Changing the negative popular perception of rats is a preoccupation of all those involved in the fancy. As well as attending shows, NFRS members also serve as public relations officers for rats. They attend agricultural events around the country and will often host a dedicated rat tent, attempting to introduce farmers and gamekeepers to a different side of the rodent. Julie Oliver has previously put in a shift at county fairs. So too, Kate Rattray, a fellow rat breeder, who has come to join us as we are chatting. Both have endured their fair share of rat hatred. 'I've had farmers coming in and saying "I'll shoot that", but on the whole people are quite understanding about it,' Kate tells me in a soft Scottish accent.

When catching a train to shows, she will sometimes encounter similar misconceptions among her fellow passengers. At first they coo at the rodents hopping around in their cage but when Kate tells them they are rats they recoil in disgust. 'I should just tell people they are long-tailed hamsters,' she says drily.

Like Julie, Kate got her first rat at university while studying for a medicine degree. She has been breeding for five or so years and will often name her rats after heavy metal bands or music lyrics. She shows me one of her rats named The Sirens are Screaming after a line in Meatloaf's 'Bat Out of Hell'.

These days Kate works as a GP. Given her profession, I ask her about rat bites. She admits that she has actually been hospitalised before from a particularly nasty nip, but blames herself entirely. When the wound became infected she initially told colleagues it was a gardening injury to avoid any further questions and so didn't receive the necessary antibiotics.

Otherwise, she and the fellow breeders I talk to say a rat bite is extremely rare. Certainly that is true from my own experience. In all the time we have had Molly and Ermintrude, they have never bitten us or anyone else playing with them.

Some breeders will take in wild rats, although their inherent suspicion of humans makes them far harder to train. Fancy rats, on the other hand, have developed a sweet and docile nature over many generations, and, crucially, hold little fear of people. A 2013 study demonstrated that rodents can inherit fear from their forebears. In the study, researchers taught male mice to associate the smell of cherry blossom with mild shocks to their feet. Their pups were then raised with no exposure to the smell, but became immediately fearful if it was introduced. The changes in the next generation were found to be physiological and psychological: they were born with both enhanced olfactory sense to detect cherry blossom and be afraid of it. The study found that these inherited painful memories were passed on by the pups to the following generation as well.

A similar inheritance has been detected in rats. One study found that male rats whose fathers had been given cocaine in laboratory experiments would ingest less of the drug than rats whose parents had no experience of the drug. This adaptation is presumed to be because their fathers have passed down genetic information that the drug is a toxin.

When she used to work as a junior doctor on hospital wards, Kate says, people were far more likely to come in with other animal bites. The statistics bear this out. Dog bites are by some distance the most common mammalian bites treated in emergency wards. One 2018 UK survey, admittedly based on a small patient sample, found that 25 per cent of people had been bitten by a dog in their lifetime, although only a third of those required treatment and fewer than 1 per cent hospital admission. A separate study has found that incidences of dog-bite admissions to hospital in England has more than doubled between 1998 and 2018, from 6.34 per cent per 100,000 people in 1998 to 14.99 per cent in 2018. Over that same time period, the study estimated, an average of 207,103 people attended accident and emergency seeking treatment for dog bites every year. Cat bites are the second most common injury, accounting for between 5 and 15 per cent of wounds inflicted by animals.

Rat-bite statistics are more difficult to come by, though according to figures released under a freedom of information request to Scotland's local health boards between 2011 and 2014, of the 10,953 animal attacks that left people requiring hospital treatment, 7,731 involved dogs and 41 cases involved rats. In 2020, meanwhile, there were 20 cases of leptospirosis recorded across England and Wales – a disease spread in the urine of infected rats (as well as mice, cows, pigs and dogs), which is extremely rare among domesticated animals.

Considering there are more than 10 million dogs in Britain, which according to the more conservative estimates is around the same number as rats, that makes the former considerably more dangerous to human health than the latter. And yet we are, broadly-speaking, a nation of dog-lovers and rat-haters.

While talking with Kate and Julie I hear a new phrase: a 'heart rat'. It is something, I'm told, that every rat owner experiences, the one rat they hold dearest no matter how many others they ultimately care for. For Julie it was Oscar, her first rat at university. Kate insists that she actually had two heart rats: a hooded rat called Horatio (which turned out to be a female and bred a surprise litter) and a Russian rex called Rebel. 'It's like a special rat,' Julie tells me. 'A rat in a lifetime.'

Perhaps it was naïve of me to assume we would visit the show and not return with a stowaway, but word soon gets around the Scawsby community hall that we are in need of some more rats. The best thing to keep a rat young, we are continually told as we chat with the breeders, is to introduce new blood.

Rats work well together. The famous seventeenth-century French fabulist Jean de La Fontaine recorded a story of two rats cooperating to hide a pilfered egg from a nearby fox. According to La Fontaine's fable, in order to protect the egg one rat lay on its back holding it with its paws, while the other dragged it home by its tail. 'After this recital, let any one who dare maintain that animals have no powers of reason,' he wrote.

In *Getting Under Our Skin*, Lisa T. Sarasohn explains how humans sought to subvert the altruistic nature of rats in order to kill them. She notes an English domestic guide called *The Vermin Killer*, published in 1780, which recommended throwing a few live rats into a pot heated over a flame. Their cries, apparently, would prompt the rest of the rats in the household to rush to their aid, meaning they too could be killed.

Various modern studies have recorded similar findings. One published in 2020 by researchers at the universities of Göttingen, Bern and St Andrews, revealed that merely the scent of a fellow rat engaged in cooperative behaviour was enough to trigger an altruistic response in other rats. They described these olfactory cues as 'the smell of cooperation'. Other studies have demonstrated conclusively that rats will eschew even highly addictive substances such as heroin in preference for social contact. Rats need other rats to keep them happy.

We are introduced to a Sheffield breeder, Lily Hoyland, who as we speak produces from behind her chair a cage containing two young rats. They are sisters, although markedly different. One is a silky black with a white belly and diamond marking on her face, and the other an agouti – the breed that most closely resembles a wild rat with chestnut, almost golden hair and a pale belly.

They will keep our elderly rats company, Lily says, and are ours for free. She insists she is happy for them to go to a good home where they will help out some fellow rats. And plus, she adds, it will save her money on feed. She tells us to come by her house and pick them up a few days later and it doesn't seem like we have much choice in the matter. As we leave, I wonder how many people walk out of Crufts with a couple of gifted dogs?

We were worried, however, about disrupting Molly and Ermintrude's peace. We had previous experience of introducing young hens into our chicken coop and it hadn't worked out well. On the first attempt at bringing in two posh pedigree chickens to keep our two rescue birds company, the animosity towards the invaders was so severe that we were forced to divide them with a wire fence. If similar fights broke out, Molly and Ermintrude wouldn't be able to cope.

Lily lives in an old stone house with a door that opens straight to the living room. We found her watching television with the two new rats, which we had decided to name Aggy and Reyta, leaping about in a carry cage on the floor. And a small dog called Karen, wearing a jumper and pink bunches in her hair.

It is late and sadly there isn't time for Lily to take us on a tour of her rat kennels in the cellar. Instead she hands over our new pets and gives us some advice on how best to introduce them. When we get home we carefully follow her instructions, thoroughly cleaning Molly and Ermintrude's cage to remove traces of their scent and then putting all four rats together in the smaller carry cage to become habituated to each other.

We hold our breath as they first race up to each other and paw one another frantically as well as rubbing their snouts close to their fur. To demonstrate she is the boss rat, Ermintrude pins down the younger two, who submit, lying flat on the bottom of the cage. They squeak and sniff and thrash around in the wood shavings. The young rats are as fast as lightning, as Molly and Ermintrude once were.

Content that no blood is going to be shed, we decide to leave them overnight. The following morning all four rats are piled up together in a sleeping huddle, a mass of coiled tails and multi-coloured fur. Somehow, I realise, as we release them back into the larger cage, we now have a colony.

CHAPTER TEN

Rat Island

Our new arrivals prompted another curious discovery. Previously, Molly and Ermintrude had always been somewhat private about their sleeping habits. During the day they had retreated to the inner confines of their pink plastic nesting box, often barricading the entrance with layers of cardboard so we could not peer inside.

Now there were four of them, the rats were suddenly emboldened to sleep outside. The new bed we had acquired from the rat show, a cushioned ledge of patterned fabric that clipped to the top of the cage, quickly became their desired sleeping spot. Our rat quartet would curl up together, their backs turned but otherwise seemingly unfazed as we walked past along the corridor.

This opened up to us a final secret world of the rats we had never been allowed to witness. We watched as they snuggled together for warmth and their bodies rose and fell with each deep, sleeping breath. So content did they seem in each other's company that the younger ones were apparently unfazed by Ermintrude's increasingly loud day-time snores.

I think of our rats and their cosy communal berth while lying awake in one of the most lonely sleeping spots I have ever been. I am by myself in a two-man tent, the only human soul on Inchcolm Island in the Firth of Forth. Across these wind-lashed, uninhabited nine hectares it is just me, the crashing waves, and the seals that have hauled themselves onto the rocky shore where they have been singing their siren songs throughout the night. These haunting cries inspired the selkie in folklore: visceral and often vengeful stories of magical transformations of seals into human form to lure people into the ocean. They sound to me part roar, part infant's wail, part plaintive, part fury.

Much closer now, I hear another more furtive sound. From immediately outside my tent comes a quiet but determined scratching. I'm suddenly very aware of the packet of dry-roasted nuts bundled up in the canvas pocket next to my head and that it is not quite correct to say it is me alone on this dark isle. For Inchcolm is also home to one of the last colonies of black rats anywhere in mainland Britain.

I wriggle out of my sleeping bag and slowly unzip the tent to check upon any unwanted intruders. It is that moment before dawn when the weather, like the selkies, blurs the boundaries between land and water and mist wreathes sea and sky. The lights of the Forth bridges blink in the distance and the illuminations of Edinburgh twinkle invitingly across the estuary. I retreat inside the tent, which I have pitched in the shadow of the twelfth-century Inchcolm Abbey, zip up the entrance as tightly as I can to deter any curious rats, and count the hours until dawn.

Black rats have long called Inchcolm home. Nobody knows for how long exactly, but certainly at least as far back as the sixteenth and seventeenth centuries when the island was used as a quarantine for merchant vessels arriving at Scotland's main ports. During this period, plague was rife among crews. Before unloading their cargo on the mainland, the ships would be forced to dock at Inchcolm to enable any disease on board to burn itself out and any infected mariners to die a slow and painful death.

In 1580, for example, the *William* (a merchant vessel) arrived in the Firth of Forth after a torrid crossing of the Baltic Sea where several crew members had died on board. According to a paper written by the Scottish historian John Ritchie, the ship's plague-stricken company of 17 sailors and 15 passengers was ordered to remain on board at Inchcolm until they were 'clengit of the said sickness'. Records show that after nine weeks on the island, the skipper and a number of other crew members had perished and the ship fallen into a state of disrepair. It took a total of 115 days for the quarantine to lift and the last survivors to be permitted to leave.

During these periods of internment, locals known as clengeris were ferried onto the island to perform sanitary tasks. Clothes were boiled or cooked in a kiln to rid them of pestilence. Cargo was scrubbed, or burned, and occasionally the ships were even temporarily scuttled to allow seawater to wash out rats from the upper decks. Inchcolm became a sanctuary for these stowaways, who had crossed the globe alongside the crews of these ships.

Present in Britain since at least Roman times, the story of the black rat, or ship rat, is comparable to that of the red squirrel, although elicits far less public sympathy. As has been the case with grey squirrels, the larger, more aggressive brown rats have out-competed the timid black rat, helping drive them to the edge of localised extinction.

The rapid domination of brown rats and displacement of their black cousins is reflected in the altered design of dovecotes in Britain from around the mid eighteenth century. Previously, the houses built by pigeon fanciers to keep their birds had nesting holes at the bottom, but this made them vulnerable to the burrowing brown rat (which was also more likely to attack birds). Instead, as the larger rodents became more prominent, the lower reaches of dovecotes were blocked with stone and lime mortar as a defence. Increasingly, dovecotes were also placed high up above buildings or built into the gable ends of homes to make it harder for brown rats to gain entrance.

Even by the twentieth century, however, black rats remained well dug in across the country and particularly so in dockyards and ports. Despite their smaller size they have also been shown to be able to coexist alongside the more domineering brown rats, using their superior climbing ability to forage above ground.

According to Professor Stephen Harris, who has studied black rats since the 1970s, their ultimate demise has been at human hands, due to our fear of their ability to spread disease and their long association with the plague. Harris has compiled an interesting history charting their rapid decline over the twentieth century and the success of eradication efforts, which also shows that in spite of everything, black rats continue to cling on. Between 1929 and 1937, he noted in a recent article for *British Wildlife*, nearly 30,000 black rats were caught in Liverpool. In the City of London in the 1930s, meanwhile, black rats made up around 90 per cent of the overall rat population.

Anticoagulant poisons and improved rat-proofing of grain shipments led to a catastrophic decline. By the twenty-first century black rats were reduced to a few colonies in docks and ports. However, as mentioned earlier in this book, they are still highly populous in other parts of the world with a warmer climate, and continue to muster regular invasions of the British Isles. In September 2022, Professor Harris urged the British Pest Control Association to survey its members, which confirmed recent sightings including at Tilbury docks, Southampton, Belfast, Felixstowe, Folkestone, Glasgow, Ipswich and Manchester.

Over the centuries, black rats have also colonised a host of islands dotted around the British coast. Often the invasive rats washed up on these far-flung shores following shipwrecks. They found an abundance of food across the islands, which form one of the world's most important breeding grounds for seabirds. Around 8 million seabirds arrive in the UK each spring and summer, some 25 different species. Rats feeding on their chicks have been shown to have calamitous consequences, with the rodents decimating populations of what are already globally threatened birds.

In recent years these last black-rat strongholds have been determinedly eliminated by conservationists to better protect nesting birds. In 2003, on Lundy in the Bristol Channel, for example, a successful campaign was launched to rid the island entirely of black and brown rats. The Lundy eradication was followed by similar attempts in the Scilly Isles. On Lamb Island, a rocky outcrop off the East Lothian coast which is owned by the psychic Uri Geller, volunteers even spent two years hunting down a single brown rat after it was picked up by an infrared camera.

One by one, black rats have been expunged from their final territories. In 2018, the Outer Hebrides archipelago, the Shiant Isles, was declared rat-free following the mass cull of a colony of black rats that had first settled there in the eighteenth century after washing up following a shipwreck. To kill the rats an estimated four tonnes of anticoagulant bait was laid across the island.

As Professor Harris notes, that left just a handful of island populations of black rats remaining around the UK: Lambay off the east coast of Ireland, and the Channel Isles of Alderney, Herm and Sark. And Inchcolm, where black rats were first officially confirmed in the 1980s, but not widely known beyond the rangers working on the island until a survey in 2019 confirmed their presence. According to the People's Trust for Endangered Species, the black rat is now one of Britain's rarest mammals.

The chance to encounter them on Inchcolm is similarly rare. The island is privately owned but cared for by Historic Environment Scotland (HES) because of ancient Inchcolm Abbey on the site. During the summer months, boat tours run daily tourist charters from the mainland. Visitors come to walk around the ruins of the abbey, established by Alexander I, who reputedly sought sanctuary after being diverted by a storm in 1123 and was given shelter by a hermit living on the island.

The tourists are only permitted a few hours of exploring before leaving again. There is a team of HES rangers posted on the island during working hours who also depart every evening for the mainland. Historically, two rangers also stayed overnight, but that ceased during the first Covid lockdown and several years later, when I am hoping to visit, is yet to resume.

My first attempts to persuade HES to allow me to camp out on the island (something I'm told nobody has officially done for 10 years) are politely, but firmly, rebuffed. However, I keep chipping away with a rat-like resolve. Eventually I am put in touch with Paul Rowlands, the area manager for the site, who fortunately seems as excited about the presence of black rats on the island as me.

Following his kind efforts intervening on my behalf, we eventually strike a deal: I am permitted to stay on Inchcolm for one night so long as I camp exactly where instructed and do not use any tent pegs in case of disturbing any ancient monuments below the ground. To counter this problem Paul will lend me some weights to ensure the tent does not blow away. And so after months of wrangling it is finally agreed. I pack my bags for Inchcolm.

Leaving my house early in the morning for the drive north I encounter a truly huge brown rat. It is 4 a.m. and I am waiting at a red traffic light on Sheffield's Chesterfield Road when its hulking form catches my eye. The rat crosses the deserted three highway lanes at a saunter. Under the yellow street-light glare its fur looks balding and mangy and its haunch muscles tighten as it lopes along. Compared to the images of black rats I have been reading up on the previous evening, it is little wonder such a formidable animal has so triumphantly assumed dominion over Britain. If I was to meet this particular creature walking home in the early hours, I too would give it a wide berth.

As I drive, the early morning radio news bulletins are also talking about rats. It is the end of August and a series of strikes have caused pile-ups of rubbish across Scotland's towns and cities. The strikes are about the cost-of-living crisis, with unions calling for pay awards for council staff to rise with inflation, but somehow all anyone on the radio seems to be discussing is the rats. People in Edinburgh have reportedly been storing their refuse in rented skips and – in the case of some apartment owners whose communal bins are overflowing – even in their bathtubs. Glasgow, in the words of one commentator, has turned into a 'rat buffet'. In Edinburgh, gulls have been sighted feasting on the rats themselves.

On arriving at South Queensferry, I see the disorder for myself. The bins lining the seafront promenade are full to the brim and stacks of rubbish bags are piled up alongside. Most have been torn to shreds by gulls, spilling out the contents onto the street. No doubt rats have also been feeding on the bins, but I have no time to investigate. After a six-hour drive I have made it just in time for the first mid-morning crossing to Inchcolm Island.

A thick fog hangs over the water, obscuring even the red steel arches of the Forth Bridge. There is already a queue of day-trippers waiting at the harbour to be ferried over to Inchcolm. A few eye my tent and large rucksack suspiciously. I smile back. I've been requested by the ferry-boat operator not to tell anyone the true purpose of my visit, for fear of putting off some of the tourists. Nonetheless, despite this secret mission, my boat ticket has still been stamped with the words 'rat surveyor'.

Steaming out across the water, I am reminded that I was here earlier in the year at the northern end of the cantilever railway bridge. I was writing then about nurdles, the tiny pellets known as mermaid's tears that form the basis of nearly every plastic product on earth and are also one of the most insidious sources of marine pollution. The environmental charity Fidra, which maps nurdle pollution, had recently published a global survey of hotspots and discovered a beach in North Queensferry that was one of the most inundated in the world.

Seabird species such as fulmars, shearwaters and puffins have all been found with nurdles in their bodies. One recent study found that 95 per cent of fulmars in the North Sea had the plastics in their stomachs; one bird had swallowed a staggering 273 pellets. Meanwhile, autopsies of puffins on the Isle of May, a vital seabird colony and nature reserve at the mouth of the Firth of Forth, found that the birds are now consuming worrying amounts of nurdles alongside their usual diet of sand eels.

Despite its long history of heavy industry, the Firth of Forth estuary is also classified as a Site of Special Scientific Interest. Over recent years, humpback whales have been spotted feeding in the water alongside minke whales and harbour porpoise. One of the secondary threats nurdles pose to these larger cetaceans is that, because of the chemical composition of the pellets, they attract other toxins in the water, acting as a toxic sponge. These so-called persistent bioaccumulating toxins can form on nurdles at concentrations millions of times higher than in surrounding water, and once ingested are slowly released into animals. Due to their rich layer of blubber, cetaceans are particularly at risk, with studies linking high levels of the toxins in whales and dolphins to cancer, immune deficiency and calf mortality.

The main motivation for ridding black rats from islands is their impact on breeding seabird colonies. It is an argument rooted in scientific fact. On Lundy, for example, 15 years after rats were removed it was reported that seabird numbers had trebled. But I wonder too how the easy win (in publicity terms at least) of taking out a species such as the rat to

benefit others somehow absolves us of responsibility. For the
nurdles are just one of countless strands of environmental
vandalism that ultimately lead back to us. We are doing
plenty enough damage without the rats.

We navigate a few rocky outcrops in the water, some with
grey seals lounging over their jagged edges and others
topped by cormorants drying their wings in the salt spray
like emblems on a Gothic coat of arms. Inchcolm lies
beyond: a horseshoe-shaped land mass whose hilly edges
sweep down into a crescent beach in the middle. At its heart
stands the medieval Inchcolm Abbey, once ruled by
Augustinian monks and now Scotland's best-preserved
cluster of monastic buildings.

After our boat docks, the tourists on board drift away
from the harbour towards the abbey. I am ushered in the
other direction. Here in the cluttered, homely office
frequented by the HES rangers I am greeted by Vikki Smith,
one of those working on the island. Filling a kettle from a
plastic bottle (there is no running water on the island), she
immediately starts talking to me about the rats. When she
first started, she says, it was something of an unspoken rule
not to mention their presence to any visitors for fear of
putting them off, but things have started to change. 'It's
because of the negative connotations around them, but
we've got a bit better talking about it now,' she says, speaking
a mile a minute. 'Rats have a terrible rep. But they are
genuinely a lovely thing to have on the island.'

When Vikki, who lives on the mainland in Fife, started
working here in the spring of 2019, she had never previously
had much contact with rats and her fellow rangers were

quick to tease her over their presence. That summer she had her first rat encounter in the bin store. 'I don't know what was the vision I had in my mind before but they are really small, cute, timid and docile and won't come at you,' she tells me, before adding with emphasis, 'They are not in any way terrifying.'

They have settled into coexistence. The rats mainly cluster around the buildings on the island, building their burrows in hedges and feeding on whatever the tourists throw in the bins. Small ice-cream tubs are their favourite, Vikki tells me, pointing out a few that have been cached in a nearby hedge. They are a nuisance in that they shred the binbags (and recently chewed through some seat covers used for weddings in the abbey). A few years ago, one rat even leapt out of a cupboard in the communal toilets and scuttled down a ranger's arm. But despite such startling encounters, none of the rangers seem to mind clearing up after them. Most visitors, meanwhile, remain in blissful ignorance that there are rats here at all.

Roughly once a year, HES commissions a team of pest controllers to monitor the buildings on the island and keep the population under control, but it is intended as a measure of control rather than annihilation. Otherwise, the rats are left to it.

Inchcolm, Vikki tells me, is prized as a site of historic interest rather than a dedicated seabird breeding colony, hence there have not yet been any concerted efforts to fully rid the island of rats. Despite their presence, many otherwise threatened birds still breed successfully here. There are about 50 pairs of puffins nesting on the island (although it is presumed without rats there could be far more), oystercatchers and eider ducks, too. A huge resident colony of herring and lesser black-backed gulls are as much of a problem for the nesting birds as anything. As well as picking off chicks, the gulls are also presumed to help keep the rats in check. They are assisted by birds of prey drifting over from the mainland. In recent years, a pair of peregrines has nested successfully on the western side of the island. The year I visit, Vikki tells me, they have fledged two chicks.

Over the centuries, a delicate ecosystem appears to have established itself between human, rat and bird, but I discover that it is now in peril. A few months previously a team of environmental surveyors arrived from the mainland to assess the black rat population. The rangers were told that an offshore windfarm was being planned at an undisclosed location and it was thought that due to the disruption it could cause to breeding seabirds, as a mitigating measure the isle of Inchcolm might have to be fully rid of its rats to help accommodate threatened birds that could move onto the island. A similar cull is also being proposed on the Channel Isle of Sark, where energy firm Ørsted has argued that its remaining black rats should be removed to help compensate for a planned 180-turbine-strong windfarm about 40 miles off Flamborough Head in Yorkshire (whose chalk cliffs are a prolific seabird breeding ground). Despite Sark being hundreds of miles away, the windfarm bosses argue the removal of rats would help boost overall populations around the British coast if the birds end up being impacted in Yorkshire. However, some Sark residents have reacted angrily to the plans, launching an impassioned defence of their black rats and describing the company's claims as 'greenwash'.

On Inchcolm I discover, somewhat to my surprise, they are similarly committed advocates for their rats. No one makes the argument more forcibly than another ranger, Rhona Aitken, who is in her first season working at the abbey. 'I would be pretty angry,' she says. 'We shouldn't be disturbing their sites. I suppose it is a balance but it seems so sad to eradicate [one of] the UK's only population at the moment. There are plenty of other rocks for seabirds.'

Rhona is not an entirely unbiased voice in the matter (if there is ever such a thing when it comes to an animal like the rat). While studying history at Edinburgh University she bought two pet rats on a whim one day on Gumtree from a seller who had discovered they were allergic to them. She named them Mina and Lucy after the two main female characters in *Dracula*. 'I thought I was very edgy, I guess,' she grins.

Her rats, she says, enjoyed the run of her student room and would often scurry off down the hallway to explore fresh territories. She taught them to spin around on their hind legs, perform a high five and navigate various rat obstacle courses. Her beloved rats were also incorrigible thieves and would often steal trinkets from around her room, as well as socks and important university papers to shred and line their nests with.

The rats were white when Rhona first acquired them, but as they grew older turned a silvery grey. They lived to nearly two and a half years and died within days of each other. The first developed a lump under her throat. Rhona spoon-fed her milk and mashed-up digestive biscuits but after her condition continued to worsen, took her to a vet who euthanised her. Without her companion, the other rat lasted only another day or so before dying in her sleep.

Rhona is yet to acquire any other rats, and to complicate matters has just moved into a small flat with her boyfriend, and his cat. She admits she still harbours ambitions of acquiring more. 'And, like, a lot more in the future,' she insists. 'At least five or six.'

As a historian she finds the presence of black rats on Inchcolm fascinating beyond their own remarkable biology. 'For me they are great as animals in themselves, but also this is their habitat now. They've been here for who knows how long and you have this continuation of history right through until now. They made it all the way to Scotland. You can see the trade and interconnectivity of the world through them. That is an aspect of globalisation I think is really interesting. Especially nowadays when people are so interested in closing borders, here is something that travelled the world.'

The summer I visit Inchcolm in 2022, the world is embroiled in fresh turmoil. The Russian invasion of Ukraine has returned war to the European continent and weaponised global energy supplies. As a major shipping route close to the oil and gas fields of the North Sea, there are plenty of reminders of this in the Firth of Forth as LPG tankers glide past the island.

Floating in the estuary is evidence of another global scourge. Vikki tells me they have been horrified to see the bodies of dead gannets washing up on Inchcolm's beaches. They are victims of a lethal and highly pathogenic strain of bird flu that has decimated seabird populations across the globe.

The remote islands scattered along Britain's coastline are among the worst affected in the avian flu epidemic. At some great skua colonies, losses of up to 85 per cent have been reported, prompting fears of an extinction-level event. Scientists monitoring Bass Rock, the world's largest colony of gannets in the Firth of Forth, normally home to 150,000 of the birds, have also recorded a collapse in populations.

Vikki tells me there have been one or two potential cases on Inchcolm, but otherwise the island has so far survived the brunt of an outbreak that is by far the worst on record.

It is a virus that has emerged on our watch as a result of intensive farming. H5N1 (the highly pathogenic strain behind this latest outbreak) was first detected on a Chinese goose farm in Guangdong Province in 1996. The following year the virus spawned in chicken farms in Hong Kong and in the early 2000s spread across neighbouring countries in South East Asia before moving into Africa, Europe, the Middle East and the US, establishing itself in both poultry farms and populations of wild birds.

In the wild, seabirds have so far borne the brunt of avian flu. Even without this deadly disease in their midst, they are creatures that already face a host of pressures. Warming seas as a result of climate change, pollution, overfishing and predation in their breeding grounds by invasive mammals such as rats have caused a precipitous decline in seabird populations, estimated by a recent University of Aberdeen study to be as high as 70 per cent over the past half-century. It is feared the additional impact of bird flu may push certain species to the brink. This is the moral quandary in which any defender of the rats remaining on islands finds themselves in. Who should have the right to remain? And what gives us the right to even choose?

By mid-afternoon the visitors have returned to the mainland. Around 4 p.m. the rangers also depart, filing along the small pier onto the last boat leaving Inchcolm. Their final act before leaving the island for the night is lowering the Saltire, which has been flying from a flagpole near the abbey, and stowing it away until the next day. As I watch this simple ceremonial task, which is presumably performed by the rangers each day, I wave goodbye and try not to think too

deeply about being marooned, attempting to reassure myself
with the thought that what could happen on an uninhabited
island populated solely by rats and ghosts?

With Inchcolm now to myself I head off on a tour of the
island. I walk up to the crumbling gun emplacements at the
east end which in the First and Second World Wars were
used as a centre point of the naval defences along the Firth
of Forth. Along the cliff path, fruiting crab-apple trees have
seeded in the cleaved rock. Near one clump of greenery, I
hear a rat-like rustle and freeze for several minutes but
nothing emerges. The closer I reach to the top of the island
the more the gulls kick up their caterwauling and swirl
alarmingly close to my head. At the height of breeding
season, when there are tens of thousands of gulls packed
onto the island, they will regularly divebomb any human
who strays into their patch.

Most of the barrack blocks and gun turrets were destroyed
by the Royal Engineers in the 1960s. It was a messy job
involving what was clearly a large amount of dynamite, but
the complications of clearing the wreckage off the island
meant they simply abandoned the rubble. At the top of the
cliff I pick my way round the few surviving buildings and
over great chunks of concrete streaked with guano and lichen.

Inchcolm's strategic location means it has always been a
contested scrap of land. In the 1500s it was used as a garrison
for English forces during Henry VIII's brutal dynastic war
known as the Rough Wooing. Prior to that, English ships
would regularly plunder the abbey. During one such raid in
1335, English forces seized the statue of St Columba (the
Irish saint venerated by the monks on Inchcolm). As the
invaders escaped with their loot, a violent storm whipped
up in the Firth of Forth. Fearing God's wrath, they sheepishly
returned the stolen icon.

Before Augustinian canons settled here in the twelfth century, Inchcolm was also home to Viking settlers, whose trading routes are thought to have precipitated a second black rat invasion into Europe from the east. A tenth-century hogback stone, a Viking grave marker, is the oldest known relic retrieved from the island, though much of Inchcolm's history from this period has yet to be excavated. Another of the island rangers, an archaeologist and bone specialist called Dave Henderson, is convinced that an undiscovered Viking burial ground lies beneath the feet of visitors.

During the First World War an extensive tramway system was built to distribute ammunition across the island and a few sections have remained. I follow one of the tracks through a narrow tunnel constructed by the Royal Engineers in 1916, which has remained intact. I promise myself as I plunge into the darkness of the century-old brickwork that I won't look behind me at whatever ghost of Inchcolm may be watching me pass.

The tunnel emerges at the bin stores where my feet crunch over a multitude of small chicken bones. Vikki had told me earlier in the day that they are discarded by the gulls that raid the bins of a branch of KFC in a shopping mall across the water before flying back to the island with their haul. Occasionally visitors enthused by Inchcolm's history will bring one of the bones over to the rangers' office, wondering if they have discovered an ancient relic worthy of preservation.

As the estuary wind whistles over the water between the igneous stacks and concrete, I think of all these layers of human history. The rocks of former civilisations and the ruins of our own. I remember reading once that the chicken bone will be humanity's most ubiquitous fossil, the one that will define our own age: key geological evidence of our own excessive consumption and despoiling of the world.

Through these various epochs, the nature on the island
has simply learned to adapt. The countless armies raised here
and the fights to rule the land mean nothing to the rats and
gulls, aside from different sources of food. The chicken bones
are merely the product of the latest brand of civilisation to
claim dominion over this island. It is a thought that makes
me question our own flawed notion of progress. What
means so much to us is all the same in the eyes of the rats.

Before nightfall, I am keen to do as much as I can to entice
my target. I have one motion-activated wildlife camera and,
following a great deal of deliberation with the rangers, have
decided the best place to put it is in the old bread ovens
beneath the abbey: a low-ceilinged cave that is pitch-black
aside from a few shafts of light pooling on the earthen floor.
It is a foreboding place where even some of the rangers do
not like to be alone, but also perfect for rats.

I hook up my camera in the middle of one of the bread
ovens, which has a small tunnel running beside it, and focus
the lens on a tray of rat bait I have brought with me in my
rucksack. I have assembled this noxious cocktail of ingredients
using advice gleaned from the many experts met over the
course of writing this book: sardine oil, peanut butter, sunflower
seeds and chicken pellets. Even wrapped in several layers of
clingfilm, it still reeks. With my camera trap in place, I leave the
labyrinthian ovens until the morning. I know this is going to
be my only chance of photographing an Inchcolm rat.

Elsewhere on the island I do what I can to catch even the
briefest of glimpses. I have a couple of mint chocolate ice-
cream tubs which I strategically place next to a few of the
bins and keep watch from a bench nearby. I also scatter

around a few piles of Liquorice Allsorts and peanuts. The setting sun turns the sandstone abbey walls gold as the heat of the day dissipates. The island is growing colder now and increasingly unfamiliar as darkness falls. I hunker down in my coat and wait.

After an hour or so something starts thrashing around in one of the binbags. It is just beyond my line of sight and every time I take a step closer, whatever is in there freezes. It has been found that dormice can stay stock still for an hour if they detect a nearby threat and their ratty cousins are blessed with similar patience. Eventually defeated – and it is far from the only time I have lost a battle of wills with a rat – I leave.

Elsewhere on the island, the rats are toying with me. I discover all the various piles of sweets I left have vanished without a trace. Another ice-cream tub I placed by a bin has been snatched into a hedge. Nearby I find the discarded lid with neat crescent-shaped holes chewed out of it. When I return to my initial takeout spot, the other ice-cream tub has disappeared altogether.

But still I wait and wander, until long after dark. I watch the lights of the mainland flicker on while the island encloses around me. Even the searing lights of the gas terminal across the water take on a homely air.

Eventually retreating to my tent, I listen to the seals singing and read by torchlight, thinking again of what Rhona told me about the rats representing a continuation of history on the island; a long shadow cast by the humans who have occupied it. On Inchcolm it is clearer to me than anywhere else I have visited researching this book that these rat stories offer a way of understanding our own history. They are animals that exist alongside us but apart, ever-present and yet unknowable enough for us to project our own stories upon them. Amid the unfamiliar night-time sounds, I also try and push to the back of my mind another story one of the rangers told me, about a wild camper who kayaked onto Inchcolm during lockdown and ended up with a rat in his tent.

As soon as it is light enough the next morning, I head down into the bread ovens to check my wildlife camera. When I turn it on there are only two new photographs and my heart sinks. Normally if it has captured anything the automatic shutter picks up a host of images. Sure enough the first photograph, taken around 11 p.m. according to the camera, is of nothing discernible in the darkness.

But then the second photograph, captured just after midnight, appears on the screen. It shows a small black rat hurtling across at full stretch. Its eyes gleam in the infrared light and its whiskers are as delicate as spiderwebs. When I check my bait I see the imprint of rat teeth smudged in the peanut butter, the briefest of nibbles and it has gone.

I am thrilled to capture my Inchcolm rat. And when the rangers arrive back on the island several hours later, they seem similarly delighted by the photograph and that my journey has not been in vain. Although nobody says it explicitly, I suspect they are also relieved that I am still here. With the long night over, suddenly their ghost stories of Inchcolm begin to tumble out. I am told about a malevolent presence that lurks in the bread ovens and a door to the abbey (once occupied by an all-male order of monks) that will not budge if a woman tries to open it. There are supposedly 70 individual ghosts haunting the island. I wonder about the first indiscernible photograph my camera picked up and what might have set it off.

I have several hours before my boat arrives to take me back to the mainland and so I walk across Inchcolm one more time. I have been told that every year between October and March the island is entirely closed to people (including any HES staff), so before I leave I want to see what the rats eat to sustain themselves when there is no longer a continual procession of humans and their waste upon which to rely. Overnight, the roosting gulls have produced a snowstorm of feathers that has settled in drifts upon the grass surrounding the abbey. On the beach where the seals have slipped back into the water, I spot a fresh wave of multi-coloured nurdles washed up on the morning tides.

Rat islands occupy something of a mythical place in our culture, shadow kingdoms where the rodents multiply. You encounter them dotted all over the world. In New York's Long Island Sound, for example, there is a barren stretch of rock known as Rat Island, a name thought to have come from escaping prisoners from nearby Riker's Island, or perhaps the former site of a typhoid hospital. Nowadays the island is supposedly devoid of rats, but the name persists.

Off the coast of Portsmouth is another Rat Island. Officially titled Burrough Island, it was given its nickname from a grisly story of rats swimming from the prison hulks moored nearby in the eighteenth and early nineteenth centuries to feed upon the remains of inmates buried there. Back in 2014, storms washed up some human bones on the island, prompting an archaeological dig, which revealed the bodies of 35 men aged in their late teens to early sixties, packed together in elm coffins pointing east to west in Christian fashion despite it not being consecrated ground. The men were buried with no possessions, indicating they might be convicts, and studies of their bones discovered a variety of health issues in keeping with prolonged captivity, including scurvy. A nineteenth-century map also refers to the island as a 'convict burying ground'.

Sometimes, Rat Islands can escape their past. In 2021, one island of the Aleutian archipelago in Alaska, which gained its name after rats washed up here from a Japanese shipwreck in the 1780s, was renamed following a successful operation to eradicate the rodents. The new name, Hawadax Island, is an Indigenous Aleut title meaning 'the island over there with two knolls'.

As I walk over Inchcolm I pick blackberries for breakfast, enjoying the salty tang of the fruit ripening in sea air. Presumably, the sweet-toothed rats similarly clamber up to reach the berries and wind-blasted crab apples. There are plenty of other food sources away from the visitor-centre bins. Every November, seals give birth here and it is presumed the rats will feast on the afterbirth left behind on the beaches. Then of course there are the chicken bones to gnaw on and the corpses of whatever dead birds wash up, or indeed anything else.

Wafting in the morning breeze are rogue strands of barley, which I'm told date back to those planted by the monks here many centuries ago. I think back to Robert C. O'Brien's *Mrs Frisby and the Rats of Nimh*, detailing the escape of a colony of rats from an experimental laboratory and their laudable aim of living a life free of humans and all the trouble we bring to this earth. All O'Brien's mythical rats want to do is find a place where they can live peacefully and independently, and no longer pillage from humans but harvest their own crops.

The many strands of our modern troubles converge for me at Inchcolm: the pestilence of bird flu, the piles of rubbish on the mainland, the plastic in the water, the violence of our past and the reminder of ongoing war in the gas tankers crossing the estuary. And I also realise, watching the swaying fronds of barley, that here the rats have found their own utopia where for six months each winter they can live self-sufficient and free of us. But even then, I suppose, just as we can never eradicate rats from our lives, so they can never truly escape the humans they have pursued through the ages. We are bound like this, joint adventurers and annihilators, wherever we wash up.

CHAPTER ELEVEN

Burrows

At the end of *The Rat: its history and destructive character*, the Victorian author James Rodwell delivers a final and damning verdict on his protagonist. At the time of the book's publication in 1858, Rodwell had been musing upon rats for the best part of 30 years, an obsession that started in childhood after a colony killed and decapitated his pet guinea pig. His book, an assortment of anecdotes of varied and occasionally dubious provenance, details a litany of outrages committed by rats: among them a songbird breeder on the banks of the river Thames whose aviaries were pillaged by rats recently flooded out of their waterside burrows.

Other charges lined up against the rat include: destroying clothes and furniture, stealing watches and jewellery, and pillaging grain stores, pigeon lofts and poultry houses. He also details the propensity of rats to spoil important paperwork such as wills and deeds, as if they are capable of erasing our very identities.

Rodwell takes into account some mitigation. He notes, for example, that their scavenging in sewers 'renders mankind a most essential service' by helping dispose of our waste. However, when rats emerge from the shadows into the world above, he writes, 'far from being man's best friend, he becomes his most daring and rapacious enemy'.

Self-preservation, Rodwell ultimately concludes, is the first and most important rule of nature. Considering the multitude of threats posed by rats, we are left with no choice. After long deliberation, he writes, 'we have tried and condemned Mr Rat'. To perpetuate humanity's existence, Rodwell argues, we are entirely justified in waging universal war.

Many of us will have decided upon a similar condemnation of a rat colony at some point. Even otherwise dedicated naturalists can quite easily find it within themselves to kill a rat. Charles Waterton, for example, who devoted much of his life to encouraging nature on his Wakefield estate and was described in his 1865 obituary by the *Illustrated London News* as 'that most genial and enthusiastic of all field naturalists', also spent an inordinate amount of time cultivating a special loathing for rats.

He mixed up porridge and treacle laced with arsenic and deployed a team of lethal ratters spearheaded by a wild margay tiger cat he had collected from his travels across the globe. 'When I am gone to dust,' he once wrote to a friend in 1839, 'if my ghost should hover o'er this mansion, it will rejoice to hear the remark that Charles Waterton effectively cleared the premises at Walton Hall of every Hanoverian rat. Young and old'.

Moral certainty drove his campaign of eradication. Waterton, who hailed from a family of Catholics, regarded the brown rat as the embodiment of conquest and persecution. His father had told the young Charles a story about how the rats first arrived in England in 1688 in the same boats that carried over the protestant William of Orange to oust the Catholic ruler James II.

This struck a chord with Waterton, who noted the simple correlation between the two. As the Hanoverians displaced Catholic families in their homeland, so the invading rodents drove out the native black rats. The latter he regarded with the same interest and affection he devoted to many other animals. Once he rode 50 miles to see a rare black rat in a cage. 'Poor injured Briton,' Waterton said of the black rat. 'Hard, indeed, has been the fate of thy family.' As for brown rats, he once dashed one against the wall by its tail crying out 'Death to all Hanoverians'.

One late summer's day, I similarly delivered a death sentence. Earlier in the year, rats had mustered under a neighbour's shed and tunnelled under a brick wall leading into our garden chicken coop. What started as occasional forays soon turned into a more concerted invasion. As the months passed we kept discovering new rat holes, some with little caches of chicken pellets stored inside.

Occasionally, if we walked stealthily across the lawn to the end of the garden, we would surprise a rat that would then either dive underground or vault up into a thick hedge flanking the wall, skittering between the branches until it reached a suitable hiding spot. Sometimes the sound of a rat leaping for cover was enough to alert me. The racket kicked up by a startled rat makes a mockery of their famous cunning. Before they eventually lie still, the rodents thrash about like scrapping lizards.

Over the course of a few evenings, I placed my wildlife camera on one of the rat runs into the coop. From the footage, we guessed that at least half a dozen or so rodents were darting by.

Generally speaking, if you keep chickens then rats will follow. Previously we had managed to keep the invaders to a minimum by managing the environment. This is by far the most effective thing you can do with any rat infestation. Otherwise, if you kill all the rats without changing anything else, a fresh colony will simply move in. To bolster our defences we filled in rat burrows whenever they appeared, trimmed back foliage surrounding the chicken coop and hoped that the tawny owls that frequented our garden at night and the sparrowhawk that occasionally rocketed by during the day could get a clear line of sight. In his *Rat* book, James Rodwell stressed the importance of natural predators of rats, including owls, describing them as 'the police of nature'.

Every evening we carried the chicken food into our greenhouse and kept the main store separate in plastic boxes in our potting shed well away from the coop. The problem, however, was that every day we had to bring the food back out again and leave it for the hens. No matter how much we tidied up after them, that guaranteed a constant supply of protein-rich pellets, if the rats adapted their behaviour and fed during the day. Which, of course, they did.

And so their colony was able to expand. Nothing on the ludicrous scale suggested by Rodwell, who estimates that in three years one pair of rats can produce 651,050 others, but the rats were becoming entrenched. I was mindful of one modern study of brown rat breeding in the wild, where researchers mapped the rodent population living in a favela in Salvador in Brazil. The average birth rate of the female rats monitored in the study was estimated at 79 pups each year.

One afternoon I spotted a large rat with bald patches on its fur nosing about outside the potting shed. I had never seen a rat venture this close to our house before and wondered if it was a male exile looking for a new home. Rats engage in dynastic wars every bit as gripping as lions. Often a previously dominant male is expelled from the colony by younger rivals and forced to seek out a different patch. Perhaps there had been a chicken coop coup?

The following morning after sighting the lone rat, I walked into the potting shed and discovered something astonishing: a pile of rubble the size of a molehill in the middle of the concrete floor. I placed the wildlife camera inside and left it overnight to discover what had moved in. The footage confirmed my suspicions. The large rat I had spotted had somehow managed to tunnel up through the floor into the shed. Closer inspection revealed it had detected a weakness in the concrete, where it was thinly applied around the base of an old lead waterpipe, and simply chewed its way through.

I plugged the new burrow with steel wool and swept up the mess, hoping the old rat would find a new home somewhere else. We didn't spot it again. Then a few weeks later I had another rat encounter that finally persuaded me to act.

It was a Sunday afternoon and I was changing a bicycle wheel on the garden patio, near to a pond I dug with my dad soon after moving in. Over the ensuing years it has become home to an array of frogs and newts. Over winter, the frogs retreat to log piles around the pond. On hot days they often shelter underneath the irises planted around the edge of the water, cooled by their reedy leaves.

As I tinkered with my bike, I heard a piercing scream. A rat had crept up through the foliage and pounced on an unsuspecting frog. I watched powerless as it clamped the frog in its jaws and dragged it through the undergrowth back to its burrow. The amphibian's nightmarish shrieks were left ringing in my ears.

Frogs are an easy target for rats. The Ancient Greek text the *Batrachomyomachia* described an epic conflict between the two species. Supposedly the book was intended as a comic riposte to Homer's *Iliad* and the word 'Batrachomyomachia' has come to mean something of a trivial altercation, although for me this attack on our frogs was anything but. Fattened on chicken pellets and expanding their territory, the rats were now threatening the garden ecosystem. I resolved something had to be done.

I killed the rats over the course of a sunny week in late September. During the day I moved the chicken food out into our garden lawn and left spring-loaded traps near the coop, baited with pellets stuffed into peanut butter. One by one the young rats were tempted out, oblivious to the threat, and tricked by the same food being placed in the location where they normally eat. In total I killed four rats, each dying with a broken back or neck in the trap.

I don't know whether this led to a wider collapse of the colony or whether they simply moved their feeding location elsewhere, but this fightback dampened our rat problems. A few months later the chickens themselves died of old age. With a food source no longer available, the surviving rats vanished.

I had put into practice the methods taught to me from the rat-catchers I had encountered over the course of writing this book. First, clean up the habitat, then block any burrows and entry points and remove the food source as best you can. If that doesn't work, as a final resort if the rat population is getting out of control, use a powerful spring-loaded trap without any poison bait that could spread to the wider ecosystem.

I admit to feeling a sense of satisfaction that I had been able to eradicate the rats so successfully, but this was tempered by shame. After all, I had encouraged them into our garden (albeit unintentionally) by putting out food for our chickens, and then wiped out their family when I deemed they were becoming a wider pest.

On some psychological level, my actions were fuelled by the likes of James Rodwell or the overblown pamphlets of the Vermin Repression Society of the early twentieth century and their talk of a 'sacred duty' to wage war on rats. I may have permitted myself an ecological justification, but I decided whether they should live or die. I killed the rats because I could.

A few months later, I travelled to the Peak District village of Eyam for bonfire night. When I arrived around 5 p.m., crowds had already packed into the main square. Drinkers thronged outside the village pub and families chattered excitedly under trees bedecked with fairy lights. The sounds of a jazz band drifted over from a nearby flat-bed truck adorned with speakers. Burning torches sold from street stalls were held aloft into the dark sky.

Then an expectant hush settled over the crowd. As more torches were lit, a 10-foot-long (3-metre) effigy of a rat was paraded along the street by a group of adults and children wearing bobble hats. The rat was constructed out of paper stretched across a willow frame. Red LED lights were its eyes and a green one denoted its nose. As the rat passed, the crowd struck up as one chanting a three-syllable roar: 'Burn the rat.'

We marched mob-like through the village. People stood smiling on their doorsteps as the procession passed, wielding their flaming torches and calling death to the rat. Eventually we reached the village bonfire, where the rat was placed upon a tower of wooden pallets. As it caught fire the chanting reached a crescendo. Finally, the crowd cheered as its body frazzled up into sparks. Watching, I wondered whether this would be deemed acceptable for any other animal in Britain?

The bonfire-night tradition is a relatively new one, starting around the mid-2000s, although it reflects Eyam's long history as a notorious plague village. The outbreak started in September 1665 and over 14 harrowing months claimed the lives of 257 people out of a population of around 700. As entire families were wiped out, a strict lockdown was imposed upon the small community, meaning nobody was allowed to enter or leave to prevent the infection spreading further.

The plague started in a small stone cottage near to St Lawrence's Church in the centre of the village, home to a tailor called Alexander Hadfield. He had ordered a bundle of cloth from London, into which had leapt fleas carrying the dreaded plague bacterium, *Yersinia pestis*. An employed hand, George Viccars, was the first death in the household. Eventually the whole family succumbed. Only Alexander's wife, Mary, survived. In total she lost 13 relatives.

Such tragic histories are painstakingly recorded across the plague cottages of Eyam. And the blame for the outbreak has always been laid at the clawed feet of the rat, hence the annual gleeful act of retribution today. However, a 2016 epidemiological analysis of the outbreak, published in the journal *Proceedings of the Royal Society B*, found that rats, in fact, were not the main culprit for spreading the disease between households. According to the study, rodents were responsible for only a quarter of the infections across Eyam, with the rest being spread between humans.

Eyam is far from the only epicentre of plague where medical historians have revised the importance of rats. During the second plague pandemic, for example, which started with the outbreak of the Black Death in 1346 and lasted to around the 1800s, there were two severe outbreaks in Iceland in the early fifteenth century that killed more than half the population. However, the earliest archaeological evidence of any rats on Iceland whatsoever isn't until the seventeenth century.

As Professor Stephen Harris points out in his history of black rats in Britain and Ireland, at the time of the second plague pandemic the rodents were actually 'rare and erratically dispersed' across Europe as a whole. Harris points to an excavation of a late fifteenth-century well in Greyfriars, London. Of the 64 animals exhumed, only six were black rats. House mice, wood mice, common shrew and water shrew were all more common.

Today in the western US where plague is endemic (and where there are several cases each year in rural locations), the disease still circulates among mammals including prairie dogs, ground squirrels, chipmunks, ferrets and rabbits. We could wipe every rat off the face of the earth, and plague would still be among us.

Not long after the rat immolation in Eyam, I bore witness to another death. This time in the cage on my first-floor landing. At first, after the introduction of Aggy and Reyta, Molly and Ermintrude had responded positively to the injection of youthful energy in their small colony, but now Molly was struggling once more.

Her movements had become increasingly leaden and slow and her once bright eyes, which previously glistened like two black currants, were now clouded and squinting. Even her body shape had changed, her head slightly sunk into her body as her spine curved with age. She did not seem in particular pain, and was still eating and drinking, but we had started to wonder whether we should take her to the vets to be euthanised.

As she grew increasingly frail, we witnessed her fellow rats caring for her. They would groom her unkempt fur and even retrieve bits of food from hard-to-access areas of the cage and bring them for her to eat. They did not fully abandon their ratty ways. If we ever tried to feed Molly a particularly choice morsel of something to keep her spirits up, another rat would quickly snatch it away. But they were clearly aware she was ailing, and doing what they could to keep her alive.

This rat-to-rat respite worked for a while. Indeed, Molly seemed to garner a late burst of strength. One morning we woke up to find her hopping between the levels of the cage almost as energetically as she had in her youth, but this turned out to be something of a last hurrah.

When the end came it was mercifully brief. She died on the same cushioned ledge we had bought from the rat show and where the colony slept together. We found her with Ermintrude cuddled close alongside. She had also pulled a scrap of cloth over her sister's lifeless form. As we carefully lifted her body out, the rats watched us silently without moving.

In a study of rat social behaviour published in 1936, scientists decided to analyse the impact of separation on rats. The researchers took laboratory rats that had been housed together in a cage and placed them at either ends of an obstacle course designed so they could see, but not reach, one another. The scientists were surprised by the diligence with which the separated rats attempted to navigate the obstacles in order to be reunited, but at the time this was put down to an innate exploratory urge rather than any social bond, which was deemed beyond their emotional range.

This dismissive view persisted for much of the twentieth century. Rat social behaviour was considered to be restricted to competition for food and sex, caring for the young, and huddling together when cold. As we are now increasingly discovering, their inner lives are actually far more rich and complex. Before Molly's death I had read, and heard, about rats grieving a departed cage mate. Now I witnessed it for myself.

While Aggy and Reyta were largely unaffected by the death of a rat they had only spent a few months with, over the following days Ermintrude became uncharacteristically withdrawn. She kept apart from the others and during the day would sleep alone. Normally the first to rush to the bars of the cage when we appeared with any food, she seemed lethargic and unresponsive.

One modern study of rat bereavement utilised something called the 'forced swim test' to analyse the emotional impact of the loss of a loved one. Rats who had formed a bond with one another were separated in order for them to believe that their cage mate had gone for good. Then they were placed in a water tank with no choice but to swim. The study found that the forcibly separated rats spent considerably more time floating on the surface rather than

swimming in the water. Those that were then reunited with
their cage mates and returned to the water tank would
suddenly swim as energetically as before – as if they once
again had something to live for.

In the days following Molly's death, Ermintrude's emotional
state appeared to visibly sink. She floated through the day
immobilised by grief. Normally clanging with noise and
activity, the rat cage lay under a pall.

I was also surprised at my own reaction to losing Molly. I
had initially taken in our rats as a writing experiment to
explore my own fears as much as anything else. Over the
years living together I had developed an unexpectedly close
attachment. As we tickled them each evening and stroked
their fur, shared scraps of our food and let them explore our
home, we had formed deep reciprocal bonds. With Molly
gone, we grieved alongside the colony. Sometimes we
wondered whether we had even become part of it.

In Jonathan Burt's *Rat*, he notes a claim by the biologist
Michael Lynch that there are two types of rat: analytic and
naturalistic. The first, he writes, is the laboratory rat, one
created by science, and the second is the wild animal we
know from our own daily experience. But to me there is a
third rat, one lodged in our cultural memory. If we can
change the stories we tell ourselves about rats, then possibly
we can also change our relationship with them.

The various rat deaths I had witnessed over those few
months encompassed the varied impact of the rodents on
our lives. The young rats I had killed in my garden
represented the long-standing war between humans and
wild colonies that threaten to invade our homes. The rat I

had seen burned in Eyam reflected their deep cultural resonance and complex place in our history. And finally the pet rat I had mourned offered a glimpse of the possibilities of inter-species relationships beyond the enmity we are led to assume is the only feasible approach to coexistence: us versus them.

I have previously described the lack of positive rat role models in literature, but there is an interesting book published in 1904 that bucks this trend. Called *The Rat*, it was written by children's author George Hewett as part of a series of animal autobiographies. Published just as the third plague pandemic was ravaging Europe and the centuries-old war on the rat was building into demands for all-out destruction, the book appears to be out of its time. Writing under the guise of a rat called Samuel, H. T., Hewett suggested a very different perspective.

The 'T' in his protagonist's initials stand for him losing half of his tail when he was two years old, and the 'H' from when he lost a paw after moving from the country to town when he was four. Hewett imagines the minefield of a rat existence, navigating constant human attempts at obliteration, and illuminates some of the rat's better qualities when few conceived they were capable of anything beyond insatiable greed and an appetite for destruction. To truly understand a rat, Hewett suggested keeping one as a pet. 'You might see the worst side of us or you might see the best,' he wrote. 'A good deal would depend on yourself, and a certain amount upon the class of rat which you happened to get.'

As with Robert C. O'Brien's *Rats of Nimh*, the ultimate dream of Hewett's fictional rat is one free of human existence. At one point Samuel, H. T. confesses to the reader: 'It is such an enormous relief to us to get rid of the dark and baleful presence of your shadow.' Maybe one day that wish will be granted. As we are currently embroiled in the world's sixth mass extinction, the lesson learned from each previous event is that usually the apex predator in charge never emerges from the other side. For a creature that is evolving at a supercharged rate beyond human capability, perhaps one day the rats will inherit the earth?

Rat grief can sometimes be fatal. When a pair have lived together for a long time, it is not uncommon for the rat left behind to follow soon afterwards, even in a matter of days. No scientific study can confirm this, but some pet-owners I have spoken to suspect the bereaved rat dies of a broken heart.

After a lost few days, however, Ermintrude finally roused herself. With two young rats scurrying about her, she was keen to reassert her position at the top of the colony. Despite her grief, the growing lump on her chest and the fact that she was now old enough to qualify for a certificate of longevity from the North of England Rat Society, she somehow regained her former vigour.

One day we switched on the vacuum cleaner and she was back moving between the floors of the cage, enlivened by its vibrating rhythms. When we let the rats out for a run along the landing, she was once again impatiently squeezing her head between the other two to ensure she would be the first to leap out of the door and scuttle back and forth along the carpet. She still continued to attempt to climb to the top of the bars of her cage, even if she constantly appeared to be on the verge of toppling off.

Absently stroking her in my lap one day, tracing my fingers along the badger stripe of darker hair running along her back, I thought back to the notion of the 'heart rat' I had been told about by the enthusiasts at the rat show – the one rat every owner cherished above all. I realised that I had found her.

Ermintrude was the first rat I ever handled, as a weeks-old infant of whom I was initially, irrationally terrified. Over the subsequent years she and her fellow rats had revealed to me the characteristics of an animal I had been assured throughout my life possessed no redeeming qualities, only a nefarious intelligence designed to exploit. But here was empathy, cooperation, mischief, fun, loyalty and resilience. I felt again those rapid, ratty heart palpitations, so much faster than my own. With each flickering beat, I touched upon the ultimate quality that has enabled her species to navigate the centuries and conquer the world. This, then, was the final lesson my rats revealed to me. Above all else, a determination to carry on.

Acknowledgements

Rats are lost without their colony and this book could not have happened without the generosity of those who guided me through the burrows. My thanks in particular to: Professors Steve Belmain and Christiane Denys, Simon Ogden at the Sheaf and Porter Rivers Trust, Paul Rowlands at Historic Environment Scotland and the rangers of Inchcolm Island, Lily Shallom at Apopo, the National Fancy Rat Society, Lilly Hoyland at Lilliput Rattery, Darin Beckett, Hannah Musterer and Karen Wickerson of the Alberta Rat Control programme and Robert and Victoria Fuller. My thanks also to the rat catchers who kindly permitted me to shadow them in their labours and talk to me about their ancient practice: Martin Kilbride, Matthew Blackwell, Craig Morris (and Monty).

I am indebted, as ever, to my wonderful Bloomsbury editors Alice Ward, Jenny Campbell and Jim Martin for bringing this book to life and for all their support over the years. Thanks also to Mari Roberts for her thoughtful and invaluable edits and all those who offered advice on early drafts: Joe Seal-Driver, Daniel Burnand, my agent Antony Harwood and my fellow rat enthusiast Jessamy Calkin.

I am most grateful to staff and colleagues at Manchester Metropolitan University, especially Dr David Cooper at the Centre for Place Writing, Professor Catherine Fletcher and Professor Steve Miles for their advice and support.

Thanks to my mum for sniffing out any spelling mistakes in proofreading and my dad for scouring the daily papers for rat-related news (and producing an excellent rodent-themed Christmas cake). And above all thanks to Liz, whose enthusiasm and affection for rats persuaded me to invite them into our lives and write this book in the first place.

The final word, however, belongs to Molly, Ermintrude, Reyta and Agatha, whose pawprints mark every page.

Further Reading

Audoin-Rouzeau, F. 2003. *Les Chemins de la Peste*. Presses de Rennes, Rennes.

Burt, J. 2004. *Rat*. Reaktion Books, London.

Camus, A. 1948. *The Plague*. Hamish Hamilton, London.

Grass, G. 1986. *The Rat*. Luchterhand, Munich.

Graves, R. 1929. *Goodbye to All That*. Penguin, London.

Hendrickson, R. 1983. *More Cunning than Man: A Social History of Rats and Men*. Stein and Day, New York.

Herbert, J. 1974. *The Rats*. New English Library, London.

Hewett, G. M. A. 1904. *The Rat (animal autobiographies)*. Adam and Charles Black, Edinburgh.

Lovegrove, R. 2007. *Silent Fields: The Long Decline of a Nation's Wildlife*. Oxford University Press, Oxford.

Matthews, I. 1898. *Full Revelations of a Rat Catcher After 25 years' Experience*. The Friendly Societies Printing Company, Manchester.

Mayhew, H. 1851. *London Labour and the London Poor*. G. Newbold, London.

O'Brien, R. C. 1970. *Mrs Frisby and the Rats of NIMH*. Atheneum Books, Los Angeles.

Orwell, G. 1938. *Homage to Catalonia*. Secker and Warburg, London.

Potter, B. 1908. *The Tale of Samuel Whiskers or the Roly-Poly Pudding*. Frederick Warne and Co., London.

Rodwell, J. 1858. *The Rat: Its History and Destructive Character*. G. Routledge and Co., London.

Sarasohn, L. T. 2021. *Getting Under Our Skin: The Cultural and Social History of Vermin*. John Hopkins University Press, Baltimore.

Sullivan, R. 2005. *Rats: Observations on the History and Habitat of the City's Most Unwanted Inhabitants*. Bloomsbury USA, New York.

Index